This is
ETERNAL
Life

Understanding the New Covenant When
Mainstream Christianity Does Not

Steven McFadden

First paperback edition March 2023

ISBN 979-8-9867527-0-9

Upstream
Publishing

To my beautiful wife, my partner in everything, you make me better.

To my children, I love you unconditionally. May you always pursue God.

Table of Contents

Introduction

I remember that empty, lost feeling I often had in my young adult years when I encountered so many contradictory beliefs surrounding salvation. How can people have so many different ideas about how salvation works when we are all reading the same Bible? Why do I get the feeling that I am not welcome to ask questions about certain biblical topics? If people really want truth, why don't they feel intrigued instead of threatened by scripture they don't understand? These are some of the questions I remember having.

It reminded me of how I felt in high school algebra. I didn't do exceptionally well in that class because I never really understood it. I am the kind of person that really needs to fully grasp the big picture if I am going to be invested and successful in the details. I need to deeply understand. I am sure I drove my sweet teacher crazy with all my questions, but I couldn't just memorize formulas and be ok with that.

I think this is why I struggled in my faith for much of my young adult years. I was trying to live out a faith that was based on the equivalent of memorized formulas, instead of operating with a deep life changing understanding of the covenant which God designed for us.

This is where my search for truth began, and despite all my weaknesses and through many ups and downs, God rewarded my struggle.

I found this information so valuable that I began writing this book with the thought that I could leave it for my children if something happened to me before they were old enough to explain it all to them. It will still serve that purpose, but maybe you or others desire to see past the deception that permeates Christendom today. If so, I hope this little book points you in the right direction, or at least causes you to search scripture for yourself.

May you have fellowship with God and therefore life.

Chapter 1

Deceived

Humans feel safe in groups. I believe God wired this into our subconscious to help us survive. Overall, it works in our favor, but what if this survival instinct could be turned against us and manipulated to cause us harm and our ultimate demise?

People group up. Look at our cities. People are stacked on top of each other. As an introvert I shiver when I think about it, but I understand why people do it. It is about opportunity, careers, and families. We benefit by being in a community and so we naturally gather together. We don't only do this with where we live; we also do this cognitively. We tend to allign ourselves with people that think like us, and we even tend to develop the same values and perspectives as the people who are closest to us. We naturally desire to fall in line. We do a lot of this subconsciously because of this deep need we have to fit safely in our group. This is all okay if you are a part of a community that is going the right direction, but what if it is not?

What if your group is steadily walking toward a cliff? If you knew that, would you be content to just walk off that cliff with everyone else? Of course not! You would remove yourself from that crowd, and if you cared about the others, you would try to get them to save themselves as well.

At the risk of sounding overly dramatic, I believe mainstream Christianity is charging toward a cliff. People are being pushed over the edge as you read this, and the craziest thing is you hardly hear a voice of warning. Why? Because the group doesn't want to hear the dissenting voices. This is how we can be in what I see as a full-blown spiritual crisis in the western church and yet hear no sirens going off. For this reason, it might make somebody like me sound crazy. I just ask that you stick with me and give me a chance. I will briefly show you in scripture what I am talking about and then allow you to run with it. Once you start to see it, you then will see it everywhere. You just need to catch a glimpse of what the masses refuse to see to get you started.

Often when we think of threats to the church, we have the tendency to think of external threats like persecution.

It's true. The world will always be the world and will always hate Christ followers. However, I am talking about something much scarier and devastatingly more dangerous to the church than persecution. What is scarier than persecution to the church?

The alteration of truth.

Before you scoff at this as hyperbole and label me as some sort of an alarmist, I want you to humor me for a moment. As heartbreaking as persecution is, it has the ability to galvanize and refine Christians and even strengthen the church as a whole. God designed his church to overcome fear and even thrive when the world is bearing down on them. The more hardship a follower of Christ faces for the name of Christ, the stronger and more emboldened they become.

However, what if our enemy also attacks in secret; not from without but from within? An enemy that slowly and methodically chips away at the truth of the faith of generation after generation. Until one day the "faith" that the church passes down to their children is no longer the faith or discipleship Christ has called us to.

What is being preached in our pulpits today is often no longer the covenant which God designed for his people. This distorted truth that is being taught now blinds many and keeps them from seeing what is real and right, and perpetuates the problem.

This is what I believe Jesus was warning about when he warned us of the wolf in the sheep's clothing. It may look and sound right, but it is devouring us from within.

Teenagers and young adults have a desire for something

that is real, life-changing, and powerful. These are all words which describe the true gospel, but because of deception, these are qualities that are lacking from "the gospel" being espoused by many today. Children are leaving the church in droves when they become young adults. People point to an outside threat pulling them away, or that we didn't do this or that event with our kids, etc. Maybe these things are true for some, but the unfortunate truth is that many never actually left the church.

They didn't leave the church because you can't quit something you never were a part of.

I don't want to sound harsh, but the truth has been so distorted that what is being passed down to the next generation is not the same discipleship which Jesus teaches. I feel comfortable saying this is happening to the majority of our western churches.

Someone may ask, how could the majority have it wrong and not notice it? Well, remember how we opened? It is in our nature to think that we have safety in numbers, but when has that ever been the case for God's people?

The Israelites who just witnessed the power of God in the parting of the Red Sea convinced Aaron, who knew better, to make an idol to worship.

Twelve spies were sent into Canaan and only two trusted God enough to pursue obedience.

Repeatedly we see God send his people prophets to

address the prevailing wind of lies which governed their lives instead of pursuing the heart of God. Those prophets were overwhelmingly rejected in their time.

Most clearly, we see this play out when Jesus clashes with the religious elite of his day. We see how far off their hearts and minds were against the backdrop of truth, which is Christ.

Look at all the terrible things that "the church" did and all the crazy stances they took in the dark and Middle Ages in the name of Christ. Those things are obviously not what God wanted.

Yes, today we live in different times, but we still share the same human nature and Satan is still using his same tactics. It may feel a little more subtle, but it can still have the same devastating consequences. You don't have to study much church history to understand that this could easily be happening to us.

Be wary of groupthink and be sure you are pursuing truth for yourself because Satan tries to alter the truth every chance he gets. He hopes you are too weak minded to break free from the current of deception that is dragging away the masses. He wants you to be blinded to the truth and to desperately hold on to the lies you have been deceived into believing.

Why is it that Satan, "the father of lies," spends his time attacking the truth? It is simple. It is because it is effective in his mission of keeping people from God. God wants you to pursue and discover truth so that you will find life, and the best way Satan can get at God is to try to keep us from finding Him. One of the more effective weapons in his arsenal is to slowly chip away at that truth so that it does not cause too much alarm. He just needs to change things enough to alter our course to the point that we don't find life.

Then, to make sure we are entrenched in the lies we carry, we have been divided up into similar but different Christian groups where each group believes something a little different and doesn't quite get along with the other groups. This polarization in our world, and especially the church, is not good for finding truth. Why? Because instead of just seeking truth at face value, we find ourselves looking at things through the lens of our group. Or even worse, we try to make sure we don't sound like some other group. So instead of letting truth be truth, we let our division and polarization alter the truth and cause us to entrench ourselves into a position that may not completely be right. Why? It's because of the need we have to please our group. Maybe this is one of the reasons Jesus prayed so fervently for our unity in the garden; he knew that the truth and the church suffer when we are divided.

I recognize that I have painted a grim picture of the state of mainstream Christianity, but I feel like in order for us to go where we want to go, we need to know where we are. If you knew me you would know that I am an optimist, and I have hope that many can overcome this. I want this generation to be the ones who rediscover the truth and power of the gospel which has been lost to so many.

Change, however, happens on an individual level and that is why I am writing this book. I don't know how many will ever read this and it is quite possible few people ever will, but maybe it will inspire change in a handful who can go on to inspire change in others.

Like change, truth is also discovered on an individual basis. What I mean by that is I don't feel like I can just hand you the truth. You must discover the truth for yourself. So, while it is tempting to be extremely thorough and hammer out every point with exhaustive references to scripture in an attempt to fend off dismissal from critics, I think that would actually hinder your progress and act as a hurdle for those who are actually seeking truth. Those who don't want to see the truth will never be convinced anyhow. Like Jesus would often imply, not everyone has ears to hear.

While I cannot totally foresee what critics will say, considering the landscape of mainstream Christianity, I assume that I will be labeled as espousing salvation by works as opposed to salvation by grace through faith and that is not true. I am espousing salvation by relationship, which is the New Covenant. In the New Covenant, grace, faith, and works are all relevant. My hope is that when you finish reading this book you have a better understanding of each of their roles and how they contribute to this covenant.

I wrote this book short on purpose. I am hoping to give

you just enough to point you in the right direction yet allow you to fill in the blanks as you study this topic for yourself. Once your eyes are open to God's structure of salvation you can't help but see it everywhere in the Bible. When you fill in all the blanks and discover it for yourself, it then will become real and clear to you like it did for me.

I just ask that you approach this book with an open mind and a heart set on finding the truth. I am not telling you to blindly believe what I have to say. I am telling you to be skeptical and test this with the scripture. Most importantly have the courage to be honest because anything less does not help anyone, except the father of lies himself.

We are going to start off with our foundational understanding of the covenant that God has made with us. If we don't understand this covenant, we will never understand salvation.

Chapter 2

Death: A Symptom of Separation

In the beginning, God created mankind. More specifically, he created Adam and Eve. Now, we do not have a lot recorded before sin entered the picture, but what we do know is this: they could not comprehend evil or sin, and therefore they did not violate their conscience in any way. Because of this, they had no guilt or shame. We use the expression "do you have no shame?" as an insult, but wouldn't it be nice to live free from shame which often stems from the guilt of sin? The only thing they knew to be wrong was the one command God gave them. Because they had no guilt of sin on their record, their relationship to God was quite unique. Scripture says God walked with them in the paradise he created for them. Before the curse, which sin brought about, it seems they also didn't have to work very hard for food or anything they needed. Also, their existence itself was or would be sustained by the tree of life which God provided. Which means they would not experience death.

When they sinned, it separated them from God. When they were separated from God they were also separated from their home with God. It separated them from the lifestyle of living with God. It separated them from life itself because God was sustaining their life.

Separation is the consequence of sin. God is holy, righteous, and just. He does not fellowship with sinfullness. We will talk more about this separation later, but for our purposes now, it is enough to acknowledge that sin separates us from God.

The root of our problem is not death. Death is merely a symptom. The root cause of death is separation; separation from a God who loves us and sustains our lives.

We have the tendency to be completely focused on obtaining eternal life or not going to hell, and yes, we should certainly consider these things. However, we often make this the ultimate apex of what Christianity will deliver to us. While we focus on our eternal fate, we see a slightly different focal point from God's perspective.

You can see this focal point from the beginning to the end, and it is that God wants to be in a good standing relationship with his people. Everything falls into place when we have that relationship restored.

When a child does something wrong and hurts their parents in the process, which following perspective do you think would be more appreciated by their parents? If the child said, "Please don't punish me, I don't want to be punished!" or if they sincerely regretted their actions and asked their parents to forgive them? I think it is obvious that any parent would prefer the latter. Why? Because it shows the child cares about more than just themselves. It shows that they truly love and care about their parents.

As disciples, if we solely focus on reward or punishment, we are taking a similar viewpoint as the child who begs to not be punished. Even worse, we may miss what is most important. We may not even comprehend what it is God is extending to us. He doesn't just want to pardon you like a governor or president pardons a convicted criminal, or a turkey in some cases. No, he wants something better than that. Something more personal. He wants you to have a real, connected relationship with him. This relationship or fellowship with God is what saves you!

Sin through Adam and Eve caused that separation between God and man, and it is from this moment in history that we can see God enact his plan to redeem us from sin and restore our relationship with him. In the next chapter we will see that this was the priority of God and the mission of Christ.

Chapter 3

Redemption Plan

As we move through time, we see God working out his plan. He makes a covenant with Abraham. He sends the law to his people. He also gives them tabernacles and the temple. As we now know, these things were all to be a picture of what was to come.

The Old Covenant was never intended to be the answer. In Hebrews and in Paul's writings, we see that the Old Covenant was to teach a lesson to mankind. It teaches us that we are incapable of doing this thing by our own strength. One of its purposes was to show us how terribly we fail at being righteous and are unable to be pleasing to God on our own.

The New Covenant, on the other hand, is to be the real answer to the real problem we have. That real problem being that we sin, and because we sin, we are disconnected from God. We cannot fix this sin problem. There is no way for we who are unrighteous to be made righteous on our own. We need to be saved from ourselves and our own inadequacies in order to have the fellowship with God that brings about life.

One of my professors shared this with our class and it made such a big impact on me that I want to share it with you. Often, ancient writers in the New Testament time frame used a literary device called an inclusio. This device worked as bookends in their writing. The writer would place a word toward the beginning of their work and the same word toward the end of their work. This would point one's attention to what is being highlighted and would act as a literary bracket for their work.

Some scholars believe Mark utilized an inclusio in the gospel he wrote. Towards the beginning of Mark, Jesus is baptized. When he comes out of the water, the text says the skies were **torn** open and the spirit of God descended upon Jesus. Then, God said, "this is my beloved son in whom I am well pleased." You have this beautiful picture of the closeness and connection between God and Jesus. If you fast forward to the end of Mark, Jesus had just died on the cross and Mark says that the curtain in the temple was **torn** in two.

This word translated as torn in English, is found at the beginning and at the end of Mark.

What do these two instances have to do with each other,

and how does it fit in the bigger picture? Let's start with the heavens being torn at Jesus' baptism.

I have watched different films made about the gospels. Often, when this moment is depicted, they show clouds that quickly separate to show a bright light. This bright light is supposedly God who was behind the clouds.

When it says the heavens were torn, we are talking about something much more significant than clouds blowing away. We are talking about that which separates our world or dimension from the dwelling place of God being torn.

This indicates that Jesus had a closeness and connection to God that nobody else had. We see that confirmed in what happens afterward as well. The Spirit descends upon Jesus and God says, "This is my beloved son, in whom I am well pleased."

We have a visual picture of the connection between Jesus and God, and we also hear the words of relationship directly spoken by God.

What does this have to do with the end of Mark when you see the temple curtain being torn open?

This curtain separated the most holy place from the rest of the temple and the world. The most holy place was actually the dwelling place of God among his people under the Old Covenant. Remember, God cannot be in the presence of sin. The only person that could ever go into the most holy place was the high priest, and he would only go there once a year to make a sacrifice for Israel. Tradition says they would even tie a rope or chain around him before he would go in. This ensured that if he had any sin in his life which had not been dealt with, they could retrieve his body if he died in the presence of God.

Under the Old Covenant, there was no avenue for true removal of sin. In essence, the sacrifices they made just pushed it all forward. It would take the work of Christ on the cross to truly take care of sin.

God dwelled among his people because he desired to be with them. However, God doesn't want to merely be in proximity of his people, he desires true fellowship. The problem is that before the sacrifice of Christ, sin still separated God from his people.

This curtain symbolized that separation.

When the curtain was torn, it indicated that something dramatic had changed. What changed? Well, Jesus just made the perfect atoning sacrifice for mankind which can truly remove our sin. Because sin can be truly removed, it is now possible for us to enjoy the closeness and connected relationship to God that he has wanted to have with us all along.

While writing about things in the temple, the Jewish historian, Josephus, described this curtain. He said that the colors and design represented our universe and embroidered on it was "all that was mystical in the heavens." The heavens were depicted on this curtain that represented the separation between us and God. Take a moment to let that sink in.

You have the heavens being torn open and God connecting to Jesus at the beginning of Mark. Then, at the end of Mark, you have the heavens being torn open again. This time it was for you and me. Because of the substitutionary work of Jesus on the cross, the "heavens" can be torn open for us in order to have a true connected relationship with God. God can now look at us and say this is my beloved child in whom I am well pleased.

This was the plan of God from the beginning. We see it being worked out through scripture. God did what he had to do to restore that connection to mankind. Why? Because he loves us. To truly comprehend redemption, we must understand this is all about relationship.

Our salvation is predicated not on our religious status before God, but on our relationship status with God.

Chapter 4
This Is Eternal Life

This concept that salvation is tied to relationship is exactly what Jesus is talking about in John 17 when he begins what is known as the High Priestly Prayer. As I mentioned earlier, this is when Jesus prays for the unity of his church. However, also found in this prayer are the words that initially shook me and started me down the path of looking at salvation differently.

John 17 1-3
When Jesus had spoken these words, he lifted up his eyes to heaven, and said, "Father, the hour has come; glorify your Son that the Son may glorify you, since you have given him authority over all flesh, to give eternal life to all whom you have given him. And <u>this is eternal life</u>, that they <u>know you</u>, the only true God, <u>and Jesus Christ</u> whom you have sent."

Take a second to just consider the wording of what he says. It's intriguing and honestly a little bizarre to us when we are not seeing salvation correctly. He says it this way on purpose. It should make us pause and ask why he says it like this. He equates salvation to knowing God and himself because that is exactly what causes our salvation: our fellowship with God through Christ.

Now, turn back a few pages to chapter 14. We find Jesus teaching about this very same principle, and if you are like me you have heard these verses hundreds of times yet didn't catch his main point. The reason is because often we are not taught Jesus' main point in this passage.

John 14:6
Jesus said to him, "I am the way, and the truth, and the life. No one comes to the Father except through me."

Often this verse is used to confirm that Christianity is the only avenue or path that leads to salvation. It is only through Jesus that we come to the Father and find life. This is all true, but if this is where we stop, I feel like we are missing Jesus' main point.

This is part of a dialogue and is not just a stand-alone statement. You see how it starts with "*Jesus said to him.*" This is important because the conversation was not about which religions lead to eternal life. Instead, Jesus is teaching them something much more profound and personal here. Let's grab the rest of our context and start back at verse 1.

John 14:1-3
"Let not your hearts be troubled. Believe in God; believe

also in me. In my Father's house are many rooms. If it were not so, would I have told you that I go to prepare a place for you? And if I go and prepare a place for you, I will come again and will take you to myself, that where I am you may be also."

Previously, well before these verses started, it is obvious that Jesus knows his time on earth is coming to an end. He has been talking to his disciples about things that are important because he recognizes this part of his ministry is ending and he is going to have to leave them.

Therefore, he starts off this conversation by saying, "*let not your hearts be troubled.*" He knows that his physical absence is going to be tough on them, so he is comforting them.

His next words are, "*Believe in God; believe also in me.*" This may feel a little disjointed, but he hasn't changed subjects at all. I think a translation that would better fit his meaning would be, if you trust God, you should also trust in me.

This is important because the words he is about to say are a big deal and he wants them to believe what he is about to tell them.

First, he talks to them about his father's house and that he is going to prepare a place for them. He then lets them know that he will personally take them there to be with him.

Yes, these are incredibly comforting and exciting words. However, Jesus isn't done, and I think the most important part is in one of the more read over exchanges we are about to see.

John 14:4
"And you know the way to where I am going."

Think about this statement for a moment. Where did Jesus say he was going? He said he was going to prepare a place for them, right? Where is he preparing them a place? In heaven. So, in this verse, Jesus tells them they know the way to heaven. How can this be possible? Do these guys know how to navigate different dimensions and can plot a course to heaven in the spiritual realm? Of course not, and Thomas is quick to bring that up.

John 14:5
Thomas said to him, "Lord, we do not know where you are going. How can we know the way?"

Basically, he is saying, we don't know where heaven is, so how could we possibly know the way to get there? That is just logical, isn't it? How can you know the way to a place you have no idea where it is at? What we find out is Jesus was somewhat baiting them. He wanted them to struggle with this statement so he could reveal to them what he wanted them to know. This is what gets us to our verse we started with.

John 14:6
Jesus said to him, "I am the way, and the truth, and the life. No one comes to the Father except through me."

Do you see what Jesus did here? He set up this whole conversation so that he can teach them and also us something very important about salvation. Thomas is saying, and the others are probably thinking, of course we don't know the way to where you are going because you are talking about going to heaven. We can't know the way! Then Jesus' response is essentially, you do know the way because you know me... I am the way, the truth, and the life.

How powerful is that? You and I can know the way to heaven if we know the person of Jesus because he is the way.

We can see that Jesus was not solely teaching on the exclusivity of Christianity. It is obviously implied, but his main focus is to get them to understand how all this works. Their relationship with him is to be their religion, because their relationship with him leads to the Father and their ultimate salvation.

Remember earlier when Jesus was talking about preparing a place for them in heaven, he said he would come back and take them to be with him so that they can be where he is. Isn't this really our only hope? Thomas was actually right. You and I don't know how to get to heaven. Our only chance is that Jesus will take us there, and Jesus only takes those whom he and the father knows. After all, Jesus said, "And this is eternal life, that they know you, the only true God, and Jesus Christ whom you have sent."

Chapter 5

I Never Knew You

My goal to this point has been to show you that God's plan for New Covenant salvation was not just to save us, but for us to have the opportunity to engage in an actual relationship with him. It is important that we think of salvation in these terms, or it can cause problems for us when we read scripture about this topic. If we don't understand this concept, then we will twist scripture in order for us to comprehend it through the lens in which we see salvation through. Let me give you an example.

Jesus tells of a judgement day scenario in Matthew 7. If we are talking about judgement day, then we are talking about where we spend eternity. Salvation is what will save us from spending eternity in hell (what we deserve), and then in turn spend eternity in heaven (what we don't deserve). So, we are talking about salvation and

Jesus is speaking to what brings about salvation. Let's look at this passage.

Matthew 7:21-23
"Not everyone who says to me, 'Lord, Lord,' will enter the kingdom of heaven, but the one who does the will of my Father who is in heaven. On that day many will say to me, 'Lord, Lord, did we not prophesy in your name, and cast out demons in your name, and do many mighty works in your name?' And then will I declare to them, 'I never knew you; depart from me, you workers of lawlessness.'"

For the longest time this was the scariest passage of the Bible to me. These are people who thought they would be going to heaven, but they were not. Why did they think they were going to heaven? Well, look at the things they did. Prophesying, casting out demons, and doing miracles is an amazing list of religious work, isn't it? I don't know about you, but I have not done any of these things. Nobody that I know has done any of these things either. I thought, if these people are not making it to heaven, then how can anyone?

What I came to realize is that this is the very question Jesus wants us to struggle with. He wants us to struggle with it, so that we will in turn search for what he is trying to teach. Jesus chose these amazing religious activities for a reason. If he chose "lesser" things, then one (especially religious leaders of the time) might say, well I can do better than that. I can do bigger and better things and then God will have to let me in. That is exactly the mindset Jesus was trying to teach against.

What is actually going on in this passage? Why do these people not have salvation? To build off what we have discussed previously, these people didn't know the way to heaven. We know this because when they learned they were not going to heaven, their defense was, did we not do this or that great religious thing in your name? What this tells us is that they put their trust in the religious activity they were doing.

Remember when we were talking about the John 14 passage and Jesus starts off by saying, "believe also in me," and I said another way of looking at it would be him saying trust in me? There was a reason he was telling them to trust him and that was because he was about to tell them he is preparing a place for them in heaven and that he will be the one to get them and take them there. They have a need to trust him personally because he will be the one to take them to heaven. He is where their confidence in heaven should lie.

These people in our passage we just looked at had trust, but they had trust in the wrong thing. They trusted the religious things they had done. They thought those things would grant them a place in heaven. They thought they knew the **way**, but they didn't know the **Way**.

Jesus said, "I am the way." Their way was to trust in religion instead of relationship and it earned them hell for eternity. This is confirmed by what Jesus says at the very end of this passage when he clearly says,

"I never knew you; depart from me, you workers of lawlessness."

When we understand this passage, we can see that Jesus is teaching exactly what we have been talking about. Our relationship with God is what causes our salvation, and it is that relationship that will get us to heaven. This doesn't have to be a scary passage to us at all. It can be a comforting passage when we know this concept and have developed a relationship with God through Jesus.

While these verses play into exactly what we have been discussing, it also brings up something else we need to talk about. Some people will take a teaching like this and say, see, it doesn't matter what we do because we don't trust in our actions, we trust in Christ. While it is true that we trust in Christ for salvation, it does not mean that our actions are invalid. How does Jesus start this teaching? He says, *"Not everyone who says to me, 'Lord, Lord,' will enter the kingdom of heaven, but the one who does the will of my Father who is in heaven."* Also look how he ends it, *"depart from me, you workers of lawlessness."*

The truth is, our works or actions are not suddenly void under New Covenant theology as so many teach. They do play a very important role in salvation. I know how this must sound to many. You have heard preachers use verses that seem so cut and dry about how works do not save us, and I myself just explained how we should trust in our relationship with God for salvation and not our activity. Yet here I am saying our works are involved in salvation. Before you call me a heretic and stop reading, I want you to give me some time to explain. Remember, we are swimming in deception which has permeated the church for generations and generations. We are needing to look at salvation through a different lens than what we have most likely been conditioned to. This is why it was so important for me to first talk about what is at the heart or core of salvation and that is relationship. Our connected relationship with the giver of life is what causes salvation. This will end up being the key for us to understand more correctly what our religious culture doesn't: the relationship between works and faith and how BOTH of those things play their own role in salvation.

Chapter 6
A Two-Way Covenant

At some length we talked about how we need to see salvation as God sees salvation, and that is as a relationship. One of the reasons this is important is that until we grasp this concept, we will not understand the framework or structure of New Covenant salvation.

In other words, many people do not understand what salvation is. Because they don't know what it is, they either don't fully understand the verses that deal with salvation, or they are easily fooled into believing things that are not true about salvation.

Because of this lack of understanding, lies have filled the void undetected by many. These lies about salvation sound appealing to us (a trademark of Satan's lies) and on the surface makes for a probable explanation of some verses.

Why is it that so many claim that the things we do have no bearing on our salvation? When we read through the New Testament, we consistently see that scripture obviously ties our actions or decisions to our eternal fate.

We don't even have to start with James 2:24 which says, "*You see that a person is justified by works and not by faith alone.*" This is an obvious connection made between our works and salvation which we will talk more about in a moment, but what about just some of the foundational teachings of Christ? When you pick up the New Testament and start reading, it doesn't take very long before you come to the sermon on the mount in the gospel of Matthew. If you believe that your actions and obedience are inconsequential to your salvation, then the teachings of Christ in the sermon on the mount are problematic.

Jesus ties our obedience or disobedience of his teachings to either spiritual blessing or judgement. A couple of examples that I think most are familiar with are when Jesus tells his disciples that their forgiveness is dependent on how they forgive others. Also, in a similar vein, he says that we will be judged by the measure we use to judge others. So, we see that our decisions or actions can impact our forgiveness and judgement. These are two concepts which certainly impact our salvation.

We are just six or so chapters into the New Testament

and we are already seeing that our actions or works are undoubtedly consequential. I know some will immediately reject this idea and will argue that these things are not impacting salvation. After all, for generations people have had to explain away these verses that tie our actions to salvation in order to maintain the framework they have been given or built up in their mind. How much better things would be if we didn't have to fight the years of deception Satan has been unleashing on the church. I wish we could go to the word, free from outside influence. I am convinced that God's plan is not difficult to understand, but that deception through the years has obscured the truth, so now we must spend time digging through lies to find the truth.

Unfortunately, before finding the full truth of the gospel, people settle for only part of the truth. Let me try to illustrate this concept through a joke of all things.

Person 1: I just flew in from across the Atlantic.
Person 2: I bet your arms sure are tired.

I know it's not the best joke, but it's the concept behind the joke that highlights how this type of deception typically works.

The reason why it is supposed to be funny is because obviously the person flew on a plane across the Atlantic, but person 2 only recognized one definition of the word "fly," acting as if they personally flew across the Atlantic. Obviously, they didn't fly across the ocean by their own power. They needed the plane to fly, but that is still flying right? Sure! This is how we always refer to this process when we travel this way. We say we flew there. While we didn't power the flight, we did have a part in the process. We decided to go, we got a ticket, we went through security, and we got on the plane. It is to be understood that the plane did the actual flying. However, both definitions of this word "fly" are valid and by context we understand which one makes sense.

Many people end up doing something similar with the concept of salvation in scripture.

Let's say our destination in this analogy is eternal life. Then let's say God and his power and grace is the plane. We obviously need the grace of God if we want to get to our destination. However, if you want to fly somewhere you have to get on the plane and stay on the plane. Yes, the grace of God flies us there, but it is also true that we must get to the airport and get on the plane.

Remember, the New Covenant is a relationship and relationships are two-way streets. A relationship is two working in concert. This is the way God designed it. Sure, God does the heavy lifting, but we are still expected to participate in this relationship.

If you focus on or ignore one side or the other, you miss the bigger picture and distort God's plan.

Let's look at how the scripture talks about both sides.

Chapter 7
Seeing Both Sides

To maintain our airplane illustration, the apostle Paul often talks about the airplane, if you will. What I mean by that, is Paul is often discusses God's involvement in our salvation and how his grace is what saves us, and if it wasn't for the grace of God, we would not have eternal life.

Let's look at probably the best-known passage from Paul dealing with this topic.

Ephesians 2:8-9
For by grace you have been saved through faith. And this is not your own doing; it is the gift of God, not a result of works, so that no one may boast.

I can see how somebody who has been deprived from seeing the full picture of salvation could read this verse and think that Paul is saying that our actions have nothing to do with our eternal life. However, what Paul is talking about is one side of salvation, which is a foundational aspect of New Covenant salvation, that many of the Jewish believers had problems grasping due to their understanding of the previous covenant. To fully understand what Paul is saying, we need to understand why he is saying it in the first place. (There is another big reason we have a problem understanding this verse and others like it and it has to do with how our Christian culture defines the word faith. We will cover that later.)

If you back up and look at the beginning of chapter 2, we see that he is describing how they were children of wrath. They were destined for hell. Then because of Christ, their status changed. They went from being destined for hell to being destined for heaven. Not only are they going to heaven now, but it says they "have been seated with Christ." Which means that they get to share in his glory and honor. How does this happen? Well, this is what verses 8-9 is about. It is only God's grace that can change your spiritual destiny in such dramatic fashion. I don't think that most of us have a problem understanding that we need the grace of God if we want this spiritual transformation. However, we are not Paul's original audience, are we?

One of the problems the early church faced that we do not face today has to do with their close proximity to the old covenant. The Judaizers were Jewish believers who tried to convince the Gentile believers that they had to also keep much of the old law if they wanted to be pleasing to God. The lens they viewed salvation through was tainted by the idea that God would only truly be pleased by the Jews. They had thought this way for so long that it was hard for them to see past this. Therefore, they were telling the Gentiles that they should keep those old laws that would make them "more Jewish" essentially.

What Paul was trying to get the early church to understand is that their salvation is not achieved through their keeping of the old law, but that status change to salvation is a result of the grace of God. However, many try to twist this verse, and others like it, to mean that our actions in general play no role in our salvation when that is not what Paul is claiming. Paul battled these same ideas in many churches and so we see similar thoughts expressed to them as well.

Romans 3:27-29
Then what becomes of our boasting? It is excluded. By what kind of law? By a law of works? No, but by the law of faith. For we hold that one is justified by faith apart from works of the law. Or is God the God of Jews only? Is he not the God of Gentiles also? Yes, of Gentiles also,

When writing to the church at Rome we see him dealing with this exact same concept. This time though, he actually says "works of the law," which is of course what he is referencing when he is having the same conversation with the Ephesians. Paul is saying that works of the law do not achieve the status change of going from an enemy of God to being destined for heaven. In other words, he is saying you can't flap your arms hard enough to fly across the Atlantic. You need to be on the plane of God's grace. Paul was talking about the actual mechanism that saves us, that causes salvation. He is emphasizing this dramatic difference between the two covenants, that being the gift of God's grace through Christ. Paul's immediate audience was not struggling with the idea that we have responsibilities in this covenant with God. Their struggle was the opposite. Therefore, Paul was not needing to stress man's need to get on the plane.

If Paul was talking about God's side of salvation in these verses, then where do we see our side of the street of salvation discussed?

Maybe the most obvious place to turn would be the book of James.

James 2:24
You see that a person is justified by works and not by faith alone.

On the surface it may sound like a stark contradiction to what Paul writes, but it clearly isn't when we understand how the New Covenant was designed.

First of all, he uses the word justified which holds much significance in this discussion and I will explain this soon.

Secondly, James is not talking about works of the law

like Paul. We know this because in this context he references some "works" and they are what you could call works of faith or works of love, not a keeping of old law to achieve righteousness.

Remember, Paul says we are saved by grace through faith. James' primary argument is that the faith that would access the grace of God, which we have established as the mechanism of salvation, must be a faith that works. I want you to see the whole context, so I am going to include most of what James has to say about this topic below.

James 2:14-24
What good is it, my brothers, if someone says he has faith but does not have works? Can that faith save him? If a brother or sister is poorly clothed and lacking in daily food, and one of you says to them, "Go in peace, be warmed and filled," without giving them the things needed for the body, what good is that? So also faith by itself, if it does not have works, is dead.

But someone will say, "You have faith and I have works." Show me your faith apart from your works, and I will show you my faith by my works. You believe that God is one; you do well. Even the demons believe—and shudder! Do you want to be shown, you foolish person, that faith apart from works is useless? Was not Abraham our father justified by works when he offered up his son Isaac on the altar? You see that faith was active along with his works, and faith was completed by his works; and the Scripture was fulfilled that says, "Abraham believed God, and it was counted to him as righteousness"—and he was called a friend of God. You see that a person is justified by works and not by faith alone.

Bear with me. I understand this is a lot to follow.

God saves us by his grace.

We have a need to access this grace.

Paul says we access grace through faith.

James says this faith which accesses grace is a faith that works, and it is in this way that we are justified by works.

The word justified means that one is proclaimed or pronounced as righteous. James isn't saying that works achieve or result in your righteousness, but instead your works of faith accessed grace. This is what Paul is saying when he says saved by grace through faith. Because you accessed God's grace through your active faith you were proclaimed righteous. It wasn't achieved.

Paul understands the New Covenant the same as James. Remember, Paul was battling a specific problem. That problem being that some thought they could be saved through the keeping of the Old Law. Paul was trying to convince them that the Old Covenant doesn't bring them into fellowship with God through Christ. See how Paul talks about these things with the Galatians.

Galatians 5:4-6
You are severed from Christ, you who would be

justified by the law; you have fallen away from grace. For through the Spirit, by faith, we ourselves eagerly wait for the hope of righteousness. For in Christ Jesus neither circumcision nor uncircumcision counts for anything, but only faith working through love.

We have stressed the relationship aspect of the New Covenant and notice the relational language Paul uses to describe this covenant. Again, he is emphasizing that you cannot earn acceptance to Christ through Old Covenant ways. As a matter of fact, Paul says to those who have fellowship with Christ, if they go back to the ways of the law, that they would sever their relationship with Christ.

They will fall from grace, he says.

Why would they fall from grace? It's because they are severed from Christ. Remember, it's our fellowship with Christ that brings life. So, if the old law is not going to work, what does? He says the answer is faith but notice how he describes this faith. Faith working through love. Faith that builds a relationship with Christ works.

This brings me to another important reason why so many misunderstand God's structure of salvation and that is because they are operating with an incomplete definition of faith.

Chapter 8
Faith Works

We usually don't give much conscious thought to how we acquire the definitions of the words we use. The reason is because we subconsciously build our understanding of words by hearing or reading the usage of those words over time. What if the culture you acquire your definition of a concept from does not use the same definition that the New Testament authors had in mind? That could be problematic, right?

We have allowed our current religious world to set the stage and lay a subconscious foundation that we all have to start from. We are usually working and operating with definitions of words that were handed to us by our culture instead of allowing the New Testament writers to define these terms for us. This topic may not sound fun, but it is vital to understand if we are going to comprehend what the New Testament writers mean when they say what they say. Words get their meaning from the definition by which the speaker is intending. We deal with this all the time and usually don't even think about it.

As a bad example, what if somebody said, "I think I am going to throw in the towel." What does that mean? Well, this is an expression that we use to mean quitting or giving up. That could be exactly what this person means. But what if the person who said this is standing in front of a dryer holding a wet towel? Now things have changed. We use the surrounding context to help us better understand what the speaker is intending. The best context we have to help define our biblical terms will be found in our bible, and not solely on our culture's general usage of a term or word today.

Mainstream Christianity is using a partial definition of the word faith. This is important because as Paul has established, it is through faith that we access grace, the mechanism of salvation. If faith is this key that unlocks grace, then we better know what faith is.

So, what is faith?

Hebrews 11:1
Now faith is the assurance of things hoped for, the conviction of things not seen.

For example, we have faith God exists. Is that what faith is? A strong belief? I think we would all agree that yes, it is a strong belief. This is pretty much where the western church stops defining the word faith, but is that where the Bible stops defining it?

I am convinced that the New Testament authors had a different, more complete understanding of this concept of faith.

James 2:19
You believe that God is one; you do well. Even the demons believe - and shudder!

James is saying great, you have belief, but guess what, the demons even believe in God. If you just believe, then what makes you better than the demons?

So, while faith is a strong belief in something, the faith we are looking for is more than that. Just a strong belief does not get us where we need to be when it comes to faith.

Let's look at the apostle John's understanding of the belief or faith that accesses the grace of God.

John 3:16
"For God so loved the world, that he gave his only Son, that whoever believes in him should not perish but have eternal life."

This is a verse that if you are working with an incomplete understanding of the belief or faith that accesses the grace of God, you might say confirms that our actions have very little importance. However, is that what John is intending when he writes this? We don't even have to leave this chapter to answer this question.

John 3:36
Whoever believes in the Son has eternal life; whoever does not obey the Son shall not see life, but the wrath of God remains on him.

Notice how this verse begins very much like John 3:16 in that it says belief leads to life. However, in this verse we see the assumption that is being made by John when he uses the word belief. If you believe, then you will obey. You will act on that belief and therefore spare yourself from the wrath of God.

Hebrews 5:9
And being made perfect, he became the source of eternal salvation to all who obey him...

Here, we see this same concept. Obedience is a clear conditional expectation for salvation.

Yes, faith leads to action/obedience. Not only does it lead to it, but the action is a part of that faith which accesses grace.

In James 2:22 he talks about Abraham saying:
You see that faith was active along with his works, and faith was completed by his works;

Faith does not merely reside in the intellect. It goes beyond that. Faith causes action. James says that Abraham's actions made his faith complete. So, by implication his faith would not be whole if he did not act appropriately. If you are familiar with Hebrews chapter 11, you know that the writer goes on to describe all the things that those people of faith did. Not just that they had belief.

In a nutshell, the New Testament defines faith as a strong belief which goes as far as to cause you to appropriately act upon that belief. Those works of faith are a part of your faith that accesses grace.

Your faith is going to show up in your actions and in your words. It will be visible or tangible in some way.

Abraham, as mentioned earlier, is elevated as a hero of faith in the bible and rightfully so. Not only that, but he is also used as an example of New Covenant salvation by both Paul and by James.

Paul talks about how Abraham received salvation outside of the law and points to the scripture that says, *"his faith was counted to him as righteousness."* Paul's goal is for the Gentiles to see how God's plan accepts them outside of the old law. New Covenant salvation comes by righteousness being proclaimed or imparted upon believers.

James also uses Abraham as an example of New Covenant salvation. He, however, has his audience look at it from a man's perspective. He says Abraham's actions, or works of faith if you will, completed his faith. So, the faith that is counted to him as righteousness produced actions. Without those actions, that faith would have been incomplete and not really faith at all.

Think for a moment about the life of Abraham. He

exemplified faith on several occasions because he believed in God and trusted in what he asked him to do. One of these big tests of faith, which Abraham passed, was when God asked him to sacrifice his son, through whom the covenant would be realized. Can you imagine being asked to sacrifice your son? Can you imagine the internal struggle he would have dealt with? He did deal with it and still planned on doing what God asked. Abraham packed what they needed, brought his son, made the journey, tied his son to the altar, and even raised the knife to kill him. Consider how hard this must have been, especially when Isaac realized that his dad was going to kill him. Could you imagine hearing the begging and pleading from someone you deeply loved as you prepared to kill them. This is somebody you spent their whole life protecting and nurturing and now you are going to be the one to take their life.

I personally could not imagine following through with something like this. He was going to though. Why? He had faith that God could and would intervene. In Hebrews it says that he believed God would be able to raise his son from the dead. He had so much faith that God would do something he was willing to obey God and follow through with what God had asked.

My question is this, did God not know that he would follow through with what he asked him to do? Why would God command him to do such a thing? If God knows peoples' hearts, didn't he already know Abraham's level of faith and know that Abraham would do what he asked? Of course, I believe God did know Abraham's heart and I don't think he surprised God by following through. God knows everything. So, what is the point of all this testing and watching Abraham do what God knew he would do in the first place?

First of all, as one of my good preaching buddies once said, God doesn't test people's faith to add anything to his knowledge. He knows how much faith you have. Most every time, the test is ultimately for the benefit of the person being tested.

Secondly, the bible is continuing to teach us this very important lesson. Faith that is not acted on is not really faith at all. Like James says, faith is not complete without the appropriate action accompanying it. God calls us to follow through and act on what we believe. This is the nature of faith; your actions always reflect your faith.

Jesus himself often spoke to the amount of, or the lack of, faith he would encounter. Phrases like this come to mind: *If you had faith the size of a mustard seed; O you of little faith; I have not seen a faith as great as this in all of Israel.* These are just a few examples of the times Jesus commented on the levels of faith he encountered.

Jesus' evaluation of their faith was always in response to something they did or said. Even though Jesus knew men's hearts, as it states in John, he never just walked up to people that were minding their own business and commented on their level of faith. No, he always reacted to an indication of their faith on the surface. I think of the four friends of the paralytic who tore a hole in a roof and lowered their friend down so he could be healed by Jesus. When this happened scripture says, "*when he saw their faith...*"

Scripture says that Jesus knew the heart of man. He knew people's thoughts, how they felt, and what they believed. Yet repeatedly, when Jesus commented or reacted to the faith of others, it was always after they showed their faith by acting on it. Why? Because faith is always acted on. Without the work or action, faith is incomplete.

These are just a few of the reasons why I think we shortchange the concept of faith if we just think of it as mere belief. Our culture may define it as just belief, but we cannot escape the fact that scripture does not. Scripture gives us a more rich and full definition of this concept of faith which includes the *works of faith*. I italicized works of faith because I think this is a key distinction which helps us wrap our mind around the New Covenant versus the old.

Maybe the clearest and most revealing teaching on this concept is taught by Jesus in just six words.

In this text we will see how God has designed New Covenant salvation and we will see how all these concepts such as grace, faith, and works play a role in our salvation.

Mark 5:24-34
...And a great crowd followed him and thronged about

him. And there was a woman who had had a discharge of blood for twelve years, and who had suffered much under many physicians, and had spent all that she had, and was no better but rather grew worse. She had heard the reports about Jesus and came up behind him in the crowd and touched his garment. For she said, "If I touch even his garments, I will be made well." And immediately the flow of blood dried up, and she felt in her body that she was healed of her disease. And Jesus, perceiving in himself that power had gone out from him, immediately turned about in the crowd and said, "Who touched my garments?" And his disciples said to him, "You see the crowd pressing around you, and yet you say, 'Who touched me?'" And he looked around to see who had done it. But the woman, knowing what had happened to her, came in fear and trembling and fell down before him and told him the whole truth. And he said to her, "Daughter, your faith has made you well; go in peace, and be healed of your disease."

Jesus says to her, "*your faith has made you well.*"

Why would Jesus say that? What does it mean that her faith has made her well? When you take a moment to think about that response, it is a bit perplexing. I think Jesus is taking an opportunity to teach us about faith and grace, and by implication, works.

There is no question in what actually did the healing. It was the power and grace of God that did the healing. God alone could do that.

Her works did not achieve healing, did they? She does

not have the capability to do such a thing. We know she didn't have the power to heal herself or she would have already done that. As a matter of fact, she had tried. She went from doctor to doctor and tried everything and spent all the money she had chasing this healing she desperately desired. There wasn't anything she could do on her own to achieve the healing.

This is the first part of what Paul talks about in our Ephesians passage when he says we are saved by grace. It is God who saves us. Just like the woman worked for her cleansing on her own and was unsuccessful, we also will be unsuccessful if we work for our salvation on our own. We need the grace of God. We need him to save us. We could never make ourselves pure and righteous enough on our own.

While we understand that it is God's grace and power that healed her, Jesus says that her faith is what made her well. Why would he say this when we all know it was God's grace that healed her? He says this because he is highlighting this process of accessing God's grace through our faith. Didn't Paul also say we access grace through faith? He and Jesus are both teaching salvation by grace through faith. Faith is the key that unlocks the door of grace.

This is where we run into a bit of a problem if we subscribe to mainstream Christianity's idea of faith and works. If we are defining faith as mere belief, which is disconnected from works, didn't this lady have the same "faith" moments before she touched his garment?

If it was her faith that healed her, as Jesus said, why wasn't she healed before she touched the garment? Why wouldn't she be healed the moment she believed Jesus could heal her?

Instead, she had a belief that if she got to Jesus, he could heal her. Then she had to figure out where he was. Jesus was on the move, so she had to intercept him somehow. Then she fought through a thick crowd that was pressing in around him. Then, ultimately, she had to come in contact with Jesus. It was after all this that Jesus said her faith had cleansed her.

A scriptural saving faith is not just belief. It is also what your belief causes you to do. Her belief caused her to act; her belief caused her to pursue Christ and to touch his garment. Therefore, like James says about Abraham, her faith was completed by her works and through that kind of faith, she accessed the grace of God and was healed. I feel like Jesus is clearly pointing to this very concept we have been discussing. Our faith is not complete until it is acted on.

This is how the teaching of Paul and James works together. They are both talking about the same salvation, they are just talking about the two different sides of salvation. We have God's side of our salvation in which he does all the actual work, and then we have our side of salvation which connects us to God's grace.

We cannot do anything on our own to achieve salvation, just like the woman could not heal herself. We just don't have the power or the ability. If we are saved, it is only by the power and grace of God this could be achieved; just like the woman needed the power of God to heal her. However, we access that grace of God by pursuing him in faith, and the bible makes clear that a faith that accesses God has to work.

Remember how I started this book? I talked about how God designed the New Covenant to be a covenant of relationship. This is our key for understanding how this all works. When we lose sight of it being about relationship, then the door is opened for us to be misled in all sorts of directions.

In Christ is an expression we see repeatedly throughout the New Testament. It may be stated a little differently from one place to another, but this concept is all over. What does it mean to be in Christ? I will talk about this in more detail later, but the New Testament describes this as our only hope. Being in this state is what brings about everything we are after as a Christian. It is what allows our sins to be forgiven. It is what allows us to be proclaimed righteous (justified). It is everything for us. One thing that you recognize as you study this concept is that this, above all, is a relationship status. This is all about our relationship to Christ.

We are going to come back to this, but I think this is an important place to mention it. In John 15, Jesus is talking about this status of abiding in him. If you read the whole chapter, you will see how he talks about how we have everything riding on our relationship status with him, but I want you to see what he says about our part of this equation in verse 9 and 10.

John 15:9-10
"As the Father has loved me, so have I loved you. Abide in my love. If you keep my commandments, you will abide in my love, just as I have kept my Father's commandments and abide in his love."

Jesus says, if you want to abide in my love then you should keep my commandments. This is interesting, isn't it? Jesus is talking about the responsibilities we have in maintaining this relationship with him.

Therefore, our understanding of what New Covenant salvation is, is very important. If we miss this relationship part, then we will miss everything.

People get so confused about faith and works and say things like, "these things we do have no bearing on our salvation because they are works, and works do not save us, only God's grace saves us."

This may sound good in mainstream Christianity, but it doesn't line up with what the Bible teaches. The truth is, the things we do or do not do, have an obvious effect on our relationship status with God, and our salvation fully depends on that relationship status. We have things we need to do in order to pursue a relationship with Christ and maintain that relationship with him. Then, because we are in Christ, God gives us salvation... something we cannot do for ourselves.

We are not earning salvation with our works, but we are

drawing near to God with what we do. We are connecting ourselves with Christ. Just like the woman who pursued Christ to be healed. She had to work to connect to Christ but once she did, he healed her.

Mainstream Christianity is so quick to cry "foul" when somebody brings up works playing a role in our salvation because many don't understand the New Covenant. They have been deceived by others and ultimately the father of lies.

Therefore, it is imperative that we are seeing New Covenant salvation for what it is... a relationship. We must pursue and maintain our relationship with God and just like any relationship it takes work. We are about to look at the major ways that God calls us to pursue him in obedience and therefore establish that relationship, and then maintain that relationship with him that gives us life.

Chapter 9

Belief

I don't think anybody would sincerely disagree with belief being tied to salvation. Instead, most people would disagree with me listing belief as a work. I will address that first, but then I want to talk to you about **why** scripture says belief is so essential, and how it ties into this whole relationship framework we have been talking about.

I understand writing about belief as a work may seem odd since most people are pitting belief against works in our churches today. However, Jesus didn't handle the concept of belief in the exact same way mainstream Christianity tends to. In John 6:29 he actually refers to belief as work.

John 6:28-29
Then they said to him, "What must we do, to be doing

the works of God?" Jesus answered them, "This is the work of God, that you believe in him whom he has sent."

Some may claim Jesus is not necessarily saying belief is a work, but instead, this is what they need to do as an alternative to working. I don't think that is solely the case, and we will see that when we look at more context a bit later. First, let's look at a different passage where Jesus addresses belief in a similar way.

John 20:24-29
*Now Thomas, one of the twelve, called the Twin, was not with them when Jesus came. So the other disciples told him, "We have seen the Lord." But he said to them, "Unless I see in his hands the mark of the nails, and place my finger into the mark of the nails, and place my hand into his side, **I will never believe**."*

*Eight days later, his disciples were inside again, and Thomas was with them. Although the doors were locked, Jesus came and stood among them and said, "Peace be with you." Then he said to Thomas, "Put your finger here, and see my hands; and put out your hand, and place it in my side. **Do not disbelieve, but believe**." Thomas answered him, "My Lord and my God!" Jesus said to him, "Have you believed because you have seen me? Blessed are those who have not seen and yet have believed."*

In this passage, we see the resolve in Thomas' heart. Even though everybody else is saying Jesus has risen, he is saying he will never believe unless he sees. That is a strong thing to say, isn't it? He didn't say he doesn't believe it; he says he will never believe it. There is a big difference between the two.

He has reason to believe, but his words express that his heart refuses to believe. He didn't just have a lack of evidence for his brain to decide to believe, his heart was decided that he wouldn't believe.

We see this highlighted when Jesus speaks to him. He says to him, "do not disbelieve, but believe." This indicates that either way, whether you believe or do not, there is a decision being made. I think Jesus speaks to the fact that belief does not only come out of evidence, but it also comes out of decision. Don't get me wrong, there needs to be some evidence to believe, but ultimately that decision is made by your heart.

If belief is a decision, then belief itself is a work, if we use that most general definition of work. It is something that comes from us. God has already given us all the reasons we need to believe intellectually. Typically, our belief problems are heart problems, not head problems.

I think we are all on the same page when I say we must believe to have eternal life, but I want us to switch gears and talk about why scripture says that is the case.

Why must we believe?

Hebrews 11:6
And without faith it is impossible to please him, for

whoever would draw near to God must believe that he exists and that he rewards those who seek him.

You usually only hear the first part of this verse referenced. Without faith it is impossible to please God. It is an important concept and is very quotable, but the thought is incomplete if we stop there. The writer of Hebrews didn't just want you to know it is impossible to please God without faith. He also wanted you to know why.

For whoever would draw near to God. What is he referencing here? He is referencing what we have been talking about for most of this book so far, this status of being connected to God in relationship. We see this expression used in other places and even James uses this phrase, *draw near to God*, to reference the same thing. It is just another way to talk about the relationship status we must have with God if we want life.

The imagery that comes with this expression is that there is a gap that exists between us and God. Considering the teachings of our modern church I think it is important to point out who is doing the drawing here. We are. We are the ones who need to be drawing near to God. There is something you need to do to close that gap between you and God. What is that?

...for whoever would draw near to God must believe that he exists and that he rewards those who seek him. He says that in order to close that gap between us and God we first must believe he exists and that he rewards

those who seek him.

I think it is really fascinating what the Spirit does through this text. Remember when we were talking about the definition of faith and that there are essentially two parts to faith? There is belief, which James says even the demons have, and then there are the appropriate actions that complete faith. Remember how we concluded that discussion? Without the works, faith isn't really the faith God calls for. In this verse, we are told we need faith to please God by drawing near to him in a relationship. Then, the writer breaks down this faith that pleases God into its two basic parts: belief and the works that complete faith. Belief in the existence of God so that we will work to seek him.

This is why belief is so important and is mentioned so often in the New Testament as a requirement for New Covenant salvation. If you do not believe in God then, of course, you are not going to be seeking or pursuing him.

Remember how this salvation or eternal life thing works? This new covenant is all about our relationship with God. If you do not believe in God or Jesus, then why would you even pursue him? You wouldn't. That gap between you and God would never close because you and I have a responsibility to draw near to him. We only do that when we are working to seek him, and you will seek him if you believe. Therefore, it is impossible to please God without faith because you will not do what God wants you to do without it.

This reminds me of a sermon Paul preaches to the Athenians in Acts 17. Now, these people were Greeks, so they did not have the scriptures or the tradition of the Jews. Paul has to take a very general approach in his sermon to them. I think his wording is interesting in this excerpt.

Acts 17:26-27
"And he made from one man every nation of mankind to live on all the face of the earth, having determined allotted periods and the boundaries of their dwelling place, that they should seek God, and perhaps feel their way toward him and find him. Yet he is actually not far from each one of us,"

I think we can see the heart of God in this text. We again see that it is God's desire for us to seek him. We also see that he is not that far from us. What does that mean?

The implication is that God is at least somewhat hidden. I have heard people ask the question, if God loves us so much why doesn't he just make himself obvious or visible to everyone? This is a valid question, but when you understand why God is hidden, you then realize how beautiful of a reason he has for doing this.

Back when I just had my two oldest kids, we had a daily routine. My oldest was 4 and her brother was 2. When I would get home from work, before I could even get the keys out of my pocket to unlock the door, our little 4-pound dog would hear me and start barking like crazy. The dog would then alert the kids that I was home. While both kids were equally excited, they would react in completely different ways. As I unlocked the door, my 2-year-old would lean against it. So, it took me a couple of minutes to open the door without knocking him over, all while the dog was still barking incessantly. When I finally got in the door, I would have to pick my son up who would do one of two things. He would hug me very sweetly or put his hands to my throat and choke me with a crazy look in his eyes. Seriously, he did do this. We have no idea where he picked this up at, and we were worried for a while it would never end. I like to think he was just so happy to see me he couldn't contain the urge to choke me to death.

While all of this was going on, my daughter would run somewhere and "hide." I put hide in quotation marks because she thought if she can't see you, then you can't see her. So sometimes I would see her legs sticking out behind the couch or she would have a blanket over her head. But if I took too long to find her, she would then start to howl like a wolf. I guess to help me triangulate her coordinates. Once I found her, she would then tell me how proud she was that I found her, and I had to pick her up and hug her. By this point, I am ready to punt our dog through the window because she is still barking like crazy and won't stop till I pick her up too.

So now I am holding one kid that is hugging me, one miniature murderer doing his best to take my life, and a dog I never really wanted to pick up. This is when I was finally able to acknowledge my wife who usually would take the opportunity to put dishes in the dishwasher or something. This all would happen pretty much every day when I would get home from work, and I wouldn't have traded it for anything in the world.

When my daughter hid from me, she was not hiding because she didn't love me or because she didn't want to see me. She wanted me to go look for her. She wanted me to seek her out. She wanted to know that I loved her enough to come find her.

When God tells us he is wanting us to seek him, he is not hiding so that he cannot be found. God wants us to seek him, and he wants us to find him. Sometimes God will even do things to get our attention to help us get back on the right track. I think the point of all of this is that you are not just going to stumble across God. You need to be intentional when you are looking for him if you want to find him.

Remember, this is about a relationship, and relationships are two-way streets. He wants you to want him enough to look for him. He wants you to be excited about finding him and drawing near to him.

The prerequisite for all of this is that we have the faith that causes us to seek him out. Therefore, it is impossible to please God without faith because without faith we will not seek him, and if we are not seeking him, we will not be near him. If we are not near God, then he is not pleased.

This is how God stays hidden from much of the world,

yet individuals find him every day. One of the many awesome promises given by God is that when we seek him with all our hearts, we will find him, because God wants to be found by us. As Paul says, "He is not far from anyone of us."

The woman we talked about, who tracked Jesus down to be healed, believed that Jesus could heal her. She had to believe in order to be healed by Jesus, because if she didn't believe, she wouldn't have searched him out. She would not have made a plan to get to him, and fought through all the people to touch his garment. She wasn't healed the moment she believed because God isn't looking for just mere belief. He is looking for belief that causes a person to act, to pursue, to close that gap between themselves and God. Then, when she did close that gap and made that connection with Jesus, that is when she was healed and cleansed.

Do you remember the verse we started this chapter with? The one in John 6, where Jesus references belief in himself as the work they should be doing. I want us to look at the bigger context of that verse right now. Jesus had just fed the 5000 and then sailed to the other side of the lake. The people were trying to find him because he could easily provide food for them. This is where we will pick it up.

John 6:25-29
When they found him on the other side of the sea, they said to him, "Rabbi, when did you come here?" Jesus answered them, "Truly, truly, I say to you, you are

seeking me, not because you saw signs, but because you ate your fill of the loaves. Do not work for the food that perishes, but for the food that endures to eternal life, which the Son of Man will give to you. For on him God the Father has set his seal." Then they said to him, "What must we do, to be doing the works of God?" Jesus answered them, "This is the work of God, that you believe in him whom he has sent."

What is all of this about? Jesus is trying to orientate them correctly. They are pursuing Jesus but not for the right reasons. They are wanting more free food. Jesus tells them that instead of working for physical food, they should be working *for the food that endures to eternal life*. What does that mean? Later, he goes on to explain to them that he is the "bread of life."

What he is saying is that they should be less concerned about chasing after that which sustains this life, and instead, pursue or seek after him because he personally sustains spiritual life.

Again, belief is what causes one to seek and pursue. Belief is not some mystical, magical substance that if you have it, you are saved, and if you don't, then you are not saved. That is superstition, not the New Covenant. Belief itself is not the goal. Instead, it is about what belief causes us to do. Just believing does not close that gap between us and God, but we will never draw near to him and close that gap if we do not believe.

Chapter 10

Confession

Confession is a great example of what belief should be leading us to. As we will see in a moment, confession is very much connected to belief. First though, I want us to look at one of the verses which ties confession to salvation.

Romans 10:9-10
because, if you confess with your mouth that Jesus is Lord and believe in your heart that God raised him from the dead, you will be saved. For with the heart one believes and is justified, and with the mouth one confesses and is saved.

What we are most likely to think of when we hear the word confess, is us confessing the bad things we have done. This is not the same confession Paul is talking about here. He is talking about saying that Jesus is who he says he is, and that he is our Lord. What we need to be sure to understand about confession though, is that it is not just about the words spoken. It is bigger than that.

Matthew 7:21
"Not everyone who says to me, 'Lord, Lord,' will enter the kingdom of heaven, but the one who does the will of my Father who is in heaven."

The person who claims or calls Jesus Lord has made a confession. They have verbalized that Jesus is their Lord, but Jesus says not everyone who does this will be saved. So, who is wrong, Paul or Jesus?

That is not a fair question, is it? This concept of confession is obviously bigger than just saying the magic words and then boom, you have salvation. Christianity is not some superstitious cult, and Paul is not saying that all the people who say these words have salvation. When he says this, he is assuming that the person confessing Jesus with their lips, is also doing so in their heart. What I am meaning, is that confession is not just claiming Jesus is Lord, but it is making Jesus Lord.

Jesus says there will be many who will call him Lord who will not be saved. Instead, who does he say will be the ones to go to heaven? He says, *"the one who does the will of my father"* is who will be saved.

Confession is when we put Christ on the throne and say, I want to do your will. You are the king, you are in charge, and I am not. This is what causes you to do the will of the father, and therefore, be one of those who Jesus says will enter the kingdom.

This is why it is so important for us to understand what confession is and what it is not.

Many will call Jesus Lord but just because you have called him Lord, does not mean that you have made him Lord. If that is the case, and we have not put Christ on the throne, then what do those words even mean? If we call Jesus Lord but we are not pursuing his will over our own, then we are merely lying.

Confession is foundational to our salvation much like how belief is foundational to our salvation. Remember how we said that belief is essential because of what it causes us to do? We must believe in God if we are ever going to pursue and make contact with him. This concept of confession is very similar. As belief leads to our pursuit of God, confession leads to our obedience of God.

As you know, the Old Law is extensive and comprehensive. If kept completely, it would have dictated much of the daily life of an Israelite. God knew it would take dedication and commitment for his people to keep the law. But, before he gave the whole law, he gave the ten commandments which is a distilled and abbreviated version of the law. The first two of those commands, which would make them the first two of over six hundred laws given to the people, were these:

1. I am the Lord your God, and you shall have no other gods before me

2. Do not create something and call it God and worship it as God.

Why were these the first two commands? I think God was laying some groundwork if you will. These are the ones to lead off with because if the people do not make him God, then why would they obey any of the commands he gives? They need to correctly understand their relationship to the lawgiver so that they will understand the importance of following the law.

Now, we are not under the law, but this same principle is alive and well and is what makes confession so foundational for salvation. It's foundational for salvation because it is foundational for obedience, and as Jesus says, *""Not everyone who says to me, 'Lord, Lord,' will enter the kingdom of heaven, but the one who does the will of my Father who is in heaven."* In this way, confession and belief are a lot alike because they are both about what they cause us to do. However, belief and confession are not only linked in that way alone. Belief should be what leads us to confession. Let's look back at some context of the verses we looked at earlier which ties confession to salvation and look at how it connects it to belief.

Romans 10:13-14
For "everyone who calls on the name of the Lord will be saved." How then will they call on him in whom they

have not believed? And how are they to believe in him of whom they have never heard? And how are they to hear without someone preaching?

We see in what Paul writes that belief is foundational because it leads to confession. This just makes sense, right? You are not going to give God the authority of your life if you do not even believe in him. However, it is possible for a person to believe and then not put Christ on the throne. They still want to pursue their own will and their own interests.

James discusses this concept without ever really naming it.

James 2:18-19
But someone will say, "You have faith and I have works." Show me your faith apart from your works, and I will show you my faith by my works. You believe that God is one; you do well. Even the demons believe— and shudder!

When James is talking about the connection between faith and works, he is in essence discussing confession, the link between belief and obedience. When we believe, we have a decision to make. Are we going to make Christ our Lord and do what he wants us to do, or are we just going to keep ourselves on the throne?

James is really talking about the importance of confession in this text and basically saying your belief is meaningless if you are not going to do the will of God. He gives us a dramatic example when he talks about the demons. When you think about it, it is a brilliant example.

The demons believe there is one true God. They have belief and James even says they act on that belief. He says they shudder. Which means they shake in fright of him. You and I know why they shake in fright, because they know who God is and they know that they are his enemies. Their belief in God produces action as it should. However, it is not the appropriate action. Why not? Because they do not confess Christ as Lord. They instead have made themselves the enemies of God by putting themselves on the throne; by doing what they want to do.

James is saying it is very possible for a person to believe and then not confess Christ as Lord. I know there are some who believe and yet fully rebel against God. However, most partially confess Christ. Meaning they don't completely give him control of their life.

A great example of this is the rich young ruler. You can read about him in Luke 18 if you would like. He comes to Jesus wanting salvation. He believes that Jesus has the words of life. We know this because using what we learned about belief earlier, we see that his belief has caused him to pursue Christ. He is doing good so far. Then Jesus tells him to keep the commands. The man says he has done these things since he was young. Two for two so far. Then Jesus tells him to sell all that he has and give it to the poor and then to follow him. This commandment from Christ is what did him in. This was too much for the rich young ruler and we see him walk away sadly.

What happened? His belief brought him to Jesus, but he couldn't completely make Jesus Lord. He couldn't delight in the will of God above his own. We can relate with him though, right? How hard would it be for you, if you were a billionaire, and God told you to give it all up for him? It would be hard. That is why Jesus follows this encounter up with a teaching on how hard it is for the rich to make it to heaven. Why? Not necessarily because they are wealthy, but because it is too easy for the rich to make money their god.

This doesn't mean it is easy for the rest of us poor or middle-class people. We still have the same tough decision to make. Are we going to trust God and put him in control of everything, or are we just going to be like the rich young ruler and obey the easier stuff, and hope that will be enough? The truth is, we know we need to give him full control if we want to call him Lord and not be liars.

When we do this, when we confess that Christ is Lord, we are making a relationship decision. Remember that all these things tied to salvation which we are called to do will be about our relationship to God. Because, like I keep saying, this is what salvation is, a relationship. When we confess Christ as our king, we are appropriately defining our relationship to God. We are the servant, and he is the master. He is the potter, and we are the clay. This is our relationship to God. Yes, he loves us deeply and dearly, but we should always approach God, recognizing that he is our God, and we serve him.

This is important for God. He delights in those who have enough self-awareness to approach him humbly and submissively. We see a theme through scripture, Old and New Testament alike, where God elevates those who humble themselves. Really this is the picture of salvation, is it not? You and I deserve hell because of our sins, but those that lay their lives down at the feet of Jesus receive life from God. Not only that, in Ephesians, Paul says we are to be seated with Christ in heaven. This is a dramatic position of honor. We go from deserving death to being seated with Christ in heaven because we humble ourselves and have done the will of God. This is what is at the heart of confession. We are laying our lives at the feet of Jesus and recognizing him as our Lord. We are declaring and acknowledging the correct framework and boundaries of our relationship to God, and we are rewarded for doing so.

Chapter 11
Repentance

The simple and dry definition of the word repentance is a change of mind. However, when you see this word used throughout scripture, it picks up more and more connotations as we go along, and we start to see that this word holds a lot of emotion. There is this realized abhorrence or disgust of a person's own actions, or a way of life, as the repentance takes place. Since we have the tendency to associate passion and emotion linguistically with the heart, the simple definition might be better said as a change of heart. I think this is what God is after when it comes to repentance.

Joel 2:12-13
"Yet even now," declares the Lord, "return to me with all your heart, with fasting, with weeping, and with mourning; and rend your hearts and not your

garments." Return to the Lord your God, for he is gracious and merciful, slow to anger, and abounding in steadfast love; and he relents over disaster.

Many people use the phrase "to turn around" as a definition for repentance, and it for sure would include that description, but repentance definitely starts in our minds and hearts first. It then produces the change in behavior. Notice how God is looking for an emotional response. I like the phrase, *rend your hearts and not your garments*. He is saying he wants this to be true, real, and even emotional for us. Repentance is not a cold reluctant agreement to be good now. Instead, it is an emotional and mental revolution in one's life that ultimately yields different behavior. Really, if we want to get at the heart of repentance, a person is not just disgusted with their actions because they are bad, they are remorseful for what their actions have done or accomplished. I will come back to this in a moment but let's lay a bit of groundwork first.

Just like the other topics we are discussing; scripture strongly ties repentance to salvation. We will look at one of these verses as we also start our discussion on why repentance is so vital for salvation.

I want to set this verse up so that we have some context. Peter is talking to the church in Jerusalem which, at this point, was made up of Jewish believers. Remember, they are trying to figure out this New Covenant salvation thing and for millennia before this, only the Jewish people were in covenant with God. In the passage before this verse, Peter is explaining to them how God has welcomed Gentiles to participate in this covenant as well as the Jews. This verse is the church's response.

Acts 11:18
When they heard these things they fell silent. And they glorified God, saying, "Then to the Gentiles also God has granted repentance that leads to life."

First of all, on the surface, we see that repentance is tied to eternal life. I could take the time to run through many other verses that do as well, but I think it would benefit us more to talk about why repentance is tied to salvation. I feel like as we discuss this, we will also conclude that it is something we need to do if we want life.

Now back to our verse. Notice how it talks about repentance. It says that God has granted them repentance. Which is essentially saying he is allowing them to repent. Does that seem kind of odd? Why would God have to allow or grant to anyone repentance? God is in control of everything, so yes, he could keep people from repenting if he would like, but I do not think that is what the church is talking about. They are not saying that God has allowed them to have a change of heart. Instead, they are saying God has allowed them to have a change of heart that results in eternal life.

I know I have said this over and over and I will probably keep saying it, but God is the one who grants spiritual life. In other words, he is allowing them to have a relationship with him. Notice what it doesn't say. It does not say repentance causes life. Instead, it says repentance *leads* to life. How does repentance lead to life? The short answer: repentance leads to God.

Think for a moment about the ministry of John the Baptist. His mission was to make a pathway for Jesus. To pave the way, so to speak. What was his ministry? He preached. What was his message? Repentance. Why was it important that John the Baptist was preaching repentance? Because Jesus was coming. Who was Jesus? Jesus was God in the flesh.

So, why is repentance so important that it impacts our relationship with God? Well to really understand repentance we need to understand sin more fully.

Remember earlier when I said we shouldn't just regret our sin, but we should regret what our sin causes? Our sin causes a problem, because to God, sin is personal.

I was recently reading some material from a marriage counselor who specializes in working with couples who have experienced infidelity. One thing that I found notable was that men and women typically cheat for very different reasons.

Men have a tendency to compartmentalize. They usually don't intend on hurting their marriage, and most men who cheat still claim to love their wives. How can this be possible? You and I both know that cheating is detrimental to a relationship. Well, men tend to separate their infidelity from their marriage. They convince themselves that they can be a good loving husband when they are home, and that when they are cheating it does not affect their marriage.

Now, whether it is the husband or wife doing this, how do you think their spouse will see it? Do you think they are fine with it? Of course not! They are not going to see their spouse's cheating separate from their marriage just because their spouse sees it that way. Because it is not separate. It directly and personally destroys the marriage. A person can think what they like, but it doesn't mean they're right. Infidelity is personal.

I am talking about this because we do something similar with God when it comes to sin. We have a tendency to compartmentalize and not even recognize how our sin destroys our relationship with God.

If you have been to church much at all, you have probably heard the statement that sin separates us from God. This is true, but this is such a dry and emotionless way to say it when we recognize how sin separates us from God. Sin separates us from God much like cheating separates us from our spouse.

We must remember what God wants. God wants a relationship with us. He wants to be close and connected with us. We spent the first part of this book talking about that being the priority of the New Covenant. However, God is holy and righteous so he cannot associate with or be in the presence of sin. When we choose sin, we don't do so in a vacuum. When we choose to sin, we are choosing to separate ourselves from God. We have chosen separation whether we realize it or not.

The emotions and feelings that lead to repentance are not merely spawned out of a recognition of sin. Instead, they are spawned from a recognition of what my sin has done. My sin has stood in the way of or has torn apart my relationship with God.

Paul, when writing to the Corinthians, talked about this feeling which leads to repentance.

2 Corinthians 7:8-10
For even if I made you grieve with my letter, I do not regret it—though I did regret it, for I see that that letter grieved you, though only for a while. As it is, I rejoice, not because you were grieved, but because you were grieved into repenting. For you felt a godly grief, so that you suffered no loss through us.

For godly grief produces a repentance that leads to salvation without regret, whereas worldly grief produces death.

I find it interesting that Paul uses the word "grief" multiple times to describe the feeling which led them to repentance. We usually use the word "guilt" to describe this feeling. We hear that all the time, "I feel guilty."

What is interesting is that the bible doesn't use the word "guilt" or any of its forms to describe this feeling. In the bible, the word guilt is almost always reserved for the status of guilt. You are either guilty or not. This is not an emotion; it is a legal status which is true or untrue.

This doesn't mean the Bible doesn't talk about the feelings associated with it because it does. I guess you know that because we just looked at one. We see it discussed in other places though, as well. King David deals with it a lot in the psalms. Probably his choice word to describe the feeling of guilt is sorrow.

It is telling that the two words used the most to describe the feeling of guilt are sorrow and grief. Sorrow is defined as "a feeling of deep distress caused by loss," and grief is defined as "deep sorrow, especially that caused by someone's death." This is incredible when you think about it. Both words indicate emotion caused by loss. Remember, these are the emotions which cause us to respond to our sin and repent. What is it we have lost which is causing this sorrow and grief? Well, the question is not what, the question is whom. Because when we chose sin, we also chose separation from God. We did experience loss; we lost our connection to God.

In that last verse Paul says this, *"For godly grief produces a repentance that leads to salvation..."*

Doesn't this wording sound a little familiar? The believers in Jerusalem said something very similar concerning repentance. They said repentance leads to life, and Paul said repentance leads to salvation. They both use that word lead. The reason repentance leads to salvation is because repentance leads you back to a good standing relationship with God. Our relationship to God is what causes life. Separation from God causes death. So, repentance leads to life because it helps mend that relationship we have severed.

We so often make repentance about the sin we are turning away from. We make our sin the focal point. While yes, repentance is turning away from sin, most importantly though, repentance is turning to God. Repentance is running back to that connected relationship with the giver of life. This is why repentance leads to life.

Chapter 12

Baptism

Maybe one of the most compelling actions of faith which is tied to our salvation is baptism. I know that the majority of American Protestants believe that baptism is not directly linked to salvation. What many have been taught about faith and works is that it is impossible for baptism to be linked to salvation. Most do not have a framework which allows their works to impact their salvation even though scripture says differently. I know you are probably tired of me mentioning this, but I want to make sure you understand where I am coming from. I am not saying the work of baptism achieves salvation. I am saying that baptism is ordained by God to be an avenue which connects us in relationship with Christ, which is who achieves the work of salvation. Baptism is a prime example of work tied to salvation. A work of faith that connects us to God, so that we can be saved by him.

The scriptural evidence tying baptism with salvation is overwhelming, but my main priority is to show you **why** it is connected to salvation. I feel like that might help you if you are having a hard time with this.

Remember what we established from the outset? New Covenant salvation is having that connected relationship to God. I started with that for a reason. We must be looking at salvation correctly if we are going to understand how these "works" have any impact on our salvation. We needed to start with the lens through which we look at salvation if we are going to now have any hope to see these works of faith clearly. One of our biggest obstacles in understanding salvation is the current teaching of mainstream Christianity.

If you were to fly into any city in the U.S. and just randomly pick a church to attend that Sunday, the odds are overwhelming that this specific church teaches that baptism is not connected to salvation. Why? Scripture makes it very clear that baptism is linked to salvation, and we will see that soon. If scripture is clear about this, then where does the teaching come from that says baptism doesn't impact salvation? The truth is the problem goes deeper than a misunderstanding about baptism. There is a more foundational misunderstanding at play and in order to make this errant concept work, anything that contradicts it must be explained away.

The bible's teaching on baptism certainly contradicts the

western churches' teachings on grace and faith. Instead of correcting the held understanding of grace and faith to aline with scripture, the obvious ties between baptism and salvation are explained away or avoided altogether.

Followers of Christ should always question whether they have aligned themselved with scripture, or are trying to conform scripture to meet their understanding.

I recognize that if you attend a church which does not teach about this topic in the same manner, then when I start listing some of these verses that tie baptism to salvation, your first instinct will be to start explaining them away. However, I ask you to hold off on that. Test what I have to say, but I want you to test it so that you will find truth, not just to prove any preconceived ideas.

Let's focus on the function of baptism. What is its job or role?

The Great Commission

Matthew 28:19-20
"Go therefore and make disciples of all nations, baptizing them in the name of the Father and of the Son and of the Holy Spirit, teaching them to observe all that I have commanded you. And behold, I am with you always, to the end of the age."

Jesus tells his disciples that their mission now is to go and make disciples. Just to make sure we are on the same page; disciples are Christ followers. We tend to use the term Christian today. However, that term does not even exist at the time Jesus gives this command.

Disciple is the word used to title Christ followers at this point.

Jesus is giving his disciples the task of making more Christ followers. How does this text say these disciples are to be made? He says disciples are made by them being baptized in the name of the Father, the Son, and the Holy Spirit, and by them observing what Jesus has taught.

Why is baptism part of the disciple making process? Let's answer this question as we continue to look at scriptures concerning baptism.

Pentecost

Not long after Jesus directed his disciples to go and make disciples, we have Peter preaching this first Christian sermon to the people in town for the Pentecost. After telling them that the one they crucified is the Messiah and Savior, they are heart broken. In our text we will see that they ask what they should do in response, and we see Peter's answer.

Acts 2:37-41
Now when they heard this they were cut to the heart, and said to Peter and the rest of the apostles, "Brothers, what shall we do?" And Peter said to them, "Repent and be baptized every one of you in the name of Jesus Christ for the forgiveness of your sins, and you will receive the gift of the Holy Spirit. For the promise is for you and for your children and for all who are far off, everyone whom the Lord our God calls to himself." And

with many other words he bore witness and continued to exhort them, saying, "Save yourselves from this crooked generation." So those who received his word were baptized, and there were added that day about three thousand souls.

These people heard the first gospel sermon and were convicted and wanted to know how to respond. Peter tells them their response should be to repent and be baptized, but he doesn't stop there. He goes on to say they should repent and be baptized for something. For what? What will happen if they do that? He says they should respond with repentance and baptism if they want to be forgiven for their sins, and not only that, they then would receive the Holy Spirit.

Why does baptism lead to the reception of the Holy Spirit?

Saul's Conversion

Saul, whom we know better as Paul, was on his way to Damascus to persecute Christians. On his way, he had an encounter with Christ, who appeared by a bright light that blinded Paul. He was led into Damascus where he was there praying for three days until Ananias came. Ananias laid his hands on Paul and his sight was restored and he was baptized. Paul recounts this story and the words of Ananias later in Acts 22.

Acts 22:16
"And now why do you wait? Rise and be baptized and wash away your sins, calling on his name."

Again, we have baptism being linked to the forgiveness of sins which makes salvation possible. We know that salvation cannot take place if we remain unforgiven for sin.

Also, if your sin remains on your record, how can God have fellowship with you? If New Covenant salvation is having fellowship with God, then there must be an answer for sin. That answer is obviously Jesus, but we access that forgiveness by identifying with him in baptism. This is how disciples are made because this is how people access the sacrifice of Christ. Also, God has fellowship with us by living in us through the Spirit, which is God. He will not do that unless the sin is taken care of. So, this is when we receive the Holy Spirit as well, which is obviously vital to our salvation. This is what our next text deals with.

John's Baptism vs Jesus' Baptism

We have a very telling and practical passage in Acts 18 and 19. I want to summarize some of it just to set the stage. Apollos is a strong believer and is very persuasive about Christ being the Messiah and he is convincing many that Jesus is who he said he was. It says that he didn't know about Jesus' baptism, and only knew the baptism of John. This is interesting, because a few verses later, Paul runs into some believers in Ephesus who were taught about Christ, but not his baptism. Let's pick up there.

Acts 19:1-5
And it happened that while Apollos was at Corinth,

Paul passed through the inland country and came to Ephesus. There he found some disciples. And he said to them, "Did you receive the Holy Spirit when you believed?" And they said, "No, we have not even heard that there is a Holy Spirit." And he said, "Into what then were you baptized?" They said, "Into John's baptism." And Paul said, "John baptized with the baptism of repentance, telling the people to believe in the one who was to come after him, that is, Jesus." On hearing this, they were baptized in the name of the Lord Jesus.

Paul observed something was wrong in the life of these believers and it prompted him to ask them if they had received the Holy Spirit. Their answer was no, they hadn't even heard of the Spirit. This is the part that I think is so telling when it comes to the importance of baptism. Paul, in response to the fact that they did not have the Holy Spirit, followed up with the logical question about their baptism. Why is it logical? Because baptism is when a disciple receives forgiveness of sins and at that point can fellowship with God. This is when God fellowships with his disciples by giving them the Holy Spirit. So, this is why Paul asked what was going on with their baptism. The even more interesting part of this, is that they were baptized previously, just not in the name of Jesus. We see how important the adherence to Jesus' command to make disciples through **his** baptism is.

Newness Of Life

Romans 6:3-5
Do you not know that all of us who have been baptized

*into Christ Jesus were baptized into his death? We
were buried therefore with him by baptism into death,
in order that, just as Christ was raised from the dead
by the glory of the Father, we too might walk in
newness of life. For if we have been united with him in
a death like his, we shall certainly be united with him
in a resurrection like his.*

Paul describes the meaning of baptism and that it is how
we identify with the death, burial, and resurrection of
Christ. He says we do this *in order that* we might walk
in newness of life. He goes on to indicate that baptism is
linked to our hope of resurrection, which is our ultimate
salvation.

The Circumcision of Christ

Colossians 2:11-12
*In him also you were circumcised with a circumcision
made without hands, by putting off the body of the
flesh, by the circumcision of Christ, having been buried
with him in baptism, in which you were also raised
with him through faith in the powerful working of
God, who raised him from the dead.*

Similar to the last passage, Paul refers to baptism as how
we identify with Christ and pass from our old selves to
our new selves. This is the moment we go from death to
life. However, he remarkably refers to baptism as how
we receive our circumcision from Christ.

There will be no way for me to overstate the significance
of this statement made by Paul. It is that strong of a

reference. It unequivocally connects baptism to salvation, but it is easy for the weight of what he is saying to be lost on us, considering how far removed we are from the Old Covenant. Remember when we talked previously about how Paul is battling Old Covenant ways of thinking in the church? He is wanting them to understand how the New Covenant works and how it is superior to their way of thinking about salvation. Circumcision was a big deal to Jews. This was a central part of their covenant with God. It said something. It said, these are my people, and I am their God. It was about their connection and relationship to their creator.

I wish we could grasp how important circumcision was to the Jew under the Old Covenant. His immediate audience would have understood. If we did, we would be overwhelmed by the significance that Paul places on baptism by saying it is when Christ performs our spiritual circumcision. Paul is expressing that baptism is the moment that we say to God that we are his, and when God says to us, you are mine. Isn't this the picture of what the New Covenant is all about? Our fellowship with God that brings about life.

In Christ

We can even be more specific about the relationship with God we realize through baptism. Whether you are male or female, you become a son of God. Why? Because sons of God are heirs of God. This is a necessary status change that must take place if we want to take part in Christ's kingdom. We see this stated very clearly in the following verse.

Galatians 3:26-27
for in Christ Jesus you are all sons of God, through faith. For as many of you as were baptized into Christ have put on Christ.

Notice in this verse that it says it is **in Christ** that we are sons of God. This phrase **in Christ**, or a variant of it, is found throughout the New Testament. Really, it's tough to even read an epistle for any length of time and not come across it. **In Christ** is a status. It is a relationship status with Christ that brings about all our spiritual blessings. It is a status that Christ made possible by going to the cross.

In Isaiah 64, it says that all our righteousness is like a pile of filthy rags. The prophet is saying that our righteousness is disgustingly inadequate. Where do we find the righteousness we need? We don't find it in a place, we find it in a person. We find it in Christ. (Rom 8:3-4, Rom 5:12-21, Rom 3:20-22, Philippians 2:7-11)

If we want to be righteous, holy, and blameless, we need the substitutionary work of Christ on the cross. Christ identified with us and took on our sin and punishment so that we could identify with him and take on his righteousness. (2 Cor. 5:21)

So, how is it that we enter this relationship status that provides everything for us?

Paul says that when we are baptized, we put Christ on. In other words, we enter that saving relationship status of being in Christ when we put on Christ in baptism.

This is God's ordained way that we become one of his. This is the avenue God designed that you and I can come into relationship with Christ. We identify with him and his death in the waters of baptism, and then we also get to identify with him in life.

This is the response to the gospel that God designed.

An Appeal to God

Deep down everybody knows that there should be a response of some kind to the gospel if we want salvation. Which means that there needs to be some sort of action taken on our part. However, the majority of our churches have a problem with this topic, because how we respond doesn't need to seem "too worky" to fit the current teachings of the mainstream church. What is less of a work in man's eyes other than baptism? The answer is prayer. So instead of baptism, prayer is suggested as the means by which we access the grace of God and salvation. Never mind that we see no such example in all the New Testament, and also is not taught by Christ or the apostles.

When you think about it, prayer is actually a work. It may seem like less of a work to us, but it is still something we do. Somebody's response to that might be, "but I am not trusting in my prayer to save me, I am trusting in God to save me." This is the same thing I would say about baptism. It is not the dunking in water that saves us. It is God who saves us when we respond to him the way he has ordained.

This is the stance Peter takes on baptism in 1 Peter 3:21:

Baptism, which corresponds to this, now saves you, not as a removal of dirt from the body but as an appeal to God for a good conscience, through the resurrection of Jesus Christ.

Peter states pretty clearly that baptism saves us, but to understand his reason why baptism is tied to salvation, we need to start with his example of how it does **not** save us. He says that the power of baptism is not in *the removal of dirt*. What does he mean by that? He is essentially saying the physical aspect and effects of baptism alone is not what causes salvation. If it was just the action of being immersed in water that saved us, then people would accidently receive salvation all the time when they dive in a pool or fall in a lake. This is not to say that the physical part of baptism is not important, but there has to be more involved if we want to create that connection with God we are longing for.

This brings us to Peter's reason why baptism does save us. He says that baptism saves us because it works *as an appeal to God for a good conscience*. What does he mean when he says that baptism is an appeal? A short definition of the word appeal is a formal request or petition. This word has a strong legal connotation in our language. We think of lawyers filing appeals which sound very dry and emotionless. However, in the Greek, there is an element of earnestly seeking tied into this word. To highlight the meaning of what Peter is saying, we could break it down like this: baptism saves us as an earnest request for God to provide a good conscience, and a good conscience only comes by true forgiveness of sin.

The power of baptism is not in our work, but baptism is the avenue through which God has determined for us to respond to the gospel. Baptism is how we request fellowship with God by identifying with his son in his death, burial, and resurrection.

***

The reason why it is so hard for many in mainstream Christianity to see this, is because of the teachings they grew up with. Our culture and teachings have tried to push baptism to the background and minimize its importance. Why? We talked about this concept earlier, but because so many have misunderstood the relationship between faith and works, they feel the need to separate them out as much as possible. It is hard for our children growing up with these teachings to escape them. However, if a person was insulated from these teachings and only derived their doctrine from the scripture, then it would be quite easy for them to grasp this concept because they have not committed themselves to a different way of thinking.

Inevitably, some will never challenge their religious world view and will make the easier choice to accuse this book of espousing a works-based salvation and dismiss what is actually being said. While I am claiming that scripture does tie works to our salvation, I am also claiming that it is bigger and more beautiful than that. We have been conditioned to think that salvation is either about faith or works, while scripture says salvation is a relationship which involves both faith and works.

Remember how we started this book. Salvation is all about our relationship and fellowship with God, and both our faith and works affect that relationship. Baptism is the avenue by which we access fellowship with God by putting on Christ. Baptism isn't a work which achieves salvation, but it is a relationship defined work of faith that allows us to fellowship with God, who does save us.

Chapter 13
Abide In Me

As we talked about baptism in the previous chapter, we brought up the status of being **in Christ**. This is a biblical reference to the fellowship with Christ that ultimately saves us. Remember that from the beginning of this book, I have underscored the importance of seeing the New Covenant and salvation as a two-way relationship because that is what God has designed it to be. If we see it any other way, then we will not understand what scripture has to say about salvation. We are trying to close the gap between us and God that our sin has caused. This connection that is made to God through Christ is what is being referenced by this status. This status is referred to a few different ways in scripture, but most of the time you will see **in Christ** or **in him**. There are a few exceptions such as John, who refs to it as "walking in the light," which we will see as we talk about that passage later. While we see this status of being in Christ throughout the New Testament, it is Jesus himself who introduces us to this concept and very thoroughly at that.

John 15:1-9

"I am the true vine, and my Father is the vinedresser. Every branch in me that does not bear fruit he takes away, and every branch that does bear fruit he prunes, that it may bear more fruit. Already you are clean because of the word that I have spoken to you. Abide in me, and I in you. As the branch cannot bear fruit by itself, unless it abides in the vine, neither can you, unless you abide in me. I am the vine; you are the branches. Whoever abides in me and I in him, he it is that bears much fruit, for apart from me you can do nothing. If anyone does not abide in me he is thrown away like a branch and withers; and the branches are gathered, thrown into the fire, and burned. If you abide in me, and my words abide in you, ask whatever you wish, and it will be done for you. By this my Father is glorified, that you bear much fruit and so prove to be my disciples. As the Father has loved me, so have I loved you. Abide in my love."

In this passage, Jesus uses the illustration of a vine and branch to teach us about this status of being **in him**. Obviously, we are not literally a branch and Jesus is not literally a vine. He is using this as imagery so that we might better understand a spiritual concept through

100

this physical illustration.

Let's first point out the obvious. If a branch is not connected to the vine it will die. We must be connected to Christ, or in other words be **in Christ,** if we want life. We need that status of fellowship with Christ if we want life because Christ is the giver of life, as we have established. Just as a vine gives life to one of its branches, he gives life to those whom he knows or has fellowship with. As I have tried to make clear to this point, the Bible says we certainly play a role in establishing that fellowship. We make that connection to Christ by obeying him and following him by faith. We have talked about those works of faith that scripture calls us to, in order to make that connection. However, notice that Jesus is not talking about making that connection. He is talking about maintaining that connection.

He is pleading with his disciples, those who have already established fellowship with Christ, to abide in him. He is asking them to stay connected to the vine. This is important for us to understand the significance of what is being said here. This relationship status that his disciples played a role in establishing, Jesus says they also play a role in maintaining it.

The majority of mainstream Christianity today teaches that once you have salvation that it cannot be undone. This means that most do not understand this relationship status of being in Christ, as Jesus teaches it.

We can see this lack of understanding in how people

talk about this topic. They say things like, "you cannot **lose** your salvation." If we **lose** our salvation, it is not like we have misplaced our keys. Salvation isn't some trivial, inanimate object. As we have established in this book, salvation is best understood as a deep intimate relationship. If we go from being saved to unsaved, we did not just lose the status of salvation, we severed our relationship with God.

This would be like a husband cheating on his wife, leaving her, and getting a divorce. Then when somebody asks what happened, his response being I misplaced my wife. Ridiculous, right? This is what I hear when somebody says, "you can't lose your salvation." I think they have no understanding of what salvation is.

Salvation is not something that is lost or found. Salvation is given to those who establish and maintain a relationship with Christ.

Jesus is talking to his disciples and telling them to maintain that relationship. If we could not sever our relationship with God, then why is Jesus stressing the importance of maintaining fellowship with him? Why warn them about something that could not happen? He wouldn't. It's obvious that this is a threat to his disciples, or this wouldn't be one of Jesus' last teachings to them before he goes to the cross.

Notice the wording in verse 9, *"abide in my love."* We see the relationship aspect of abiding in Christ.

If we are responsible for maintaining this fellowship with

Christ, the question is, how do we do this? How do we maintain this status of being in Christ which ultimately gives us life? Well, Jesus tells us. He is not going to tell us to abide in him, our only hope for salvation, and then not tell us how to do so. Take a look at the next verse.

John 15:10
"If you keep my commandments, you will abide in my love, just as I have kept my Father's commandments and abide in his love."

He says our obedience to him is what maintains our relationship to him. We abide in his love by keeping his commands. This should not be surprising to us when we understand how we engaged in this relationship in the first place. By faith, disciples pursued Christ through their decisions, works of faith, and obedience to his plan, so it makes sense that disciples maintain this status by their continued obedience to the teachings of Christ.

I heard a famous preacher once say that God won't let anyone lose their salvation because it would give God a bad name and he is not going to do that.

What gives God a bad name is distorting his plan of salvation and giving a false hope to millions of people who go on to believe these lies.

God is certainly loving and faithful, but he demands our love and faithfulness as well. He does not force himself on us. This is the parable of the prodigal son, is it not? The son basically wishes his father dead by requesting his inheritance when he did. Then he leaves, so that he might live the way he wants on his own. When he comes home, he is richly welcomed back. Notice what the father, who is God in this parable, says. He says that the son was dead and is now alive, was lost but now is found. This is said twice in this parable. He was a part of the household, but he decided to break his relationship with his family and leave, and Christ said he was dead and lost. Seems pretty clear what the implications are.

Salvation comes through a relationship, and relationships are a two-way street. Yes, we are saved by God's grace, but God only saves those who are in Christ. In order to be in Christ, you must initiate and maintain that relationship by complying with God's terms and conditions.

Every healthy relationship has appropriate boundaries, and God's new covenant is no different. However, many people disregarded the boundaries God set in place for this relationship. They taught people there is no need to pursue fellowship with God in order to have salvation. To top it off, they also taught that there is no possible way to lose this counterfeit salvation. It is so sad to think that anybody would be deceived in this manner, but the fact that the majority of western Christendom has seemingly fallen for this way of thinking is devastating.

I recognize that this book will not make me popular. I understand that those who espouse that salvation is simply claimed and cannot be "lost," will probably say that I am pushing a works-based salvation. Those who claim that we are saved by works will not like that I emphatically state that we are saved by the grace of God. I don't see myself in either one of these camps exclusively, but I also don't see myself as being somewhere in between. I see myself as belonging to a separate camp, the saved by relationship camp. The Bible says we are saved by grace, and it also says we are justified by works, and both are valid realities in God's two-way street covenant that he has designed.

When Jesus said that we maintain this fellowship through obedience, he is pointing to one of the more important parts of discipleship. As a disciple it is our job to follow our rabbi, our teacher, and our king, Jesus Christ. This is what confession is all about, which we talked about previously. We either make Christ king and obey him completely, or we do not. Jesus is saying your obedience to him is what allows you to abide in his love. In other words, your decisions and choices play a part in maintaining this relationship to Christ, which brings about your salvation.

When Jesus talks about keeping his commands, he is ultimately talking about our responsibility to yield our will to him. Notice how in this verse Jesus says we are to obey Christ like he has obeyed God. This is not the only place we see Jesus talk about his obedience to the Father, or that he has yielded his will to him.

John 6:38
"For I have come down from heaven, not to do my own will but the will of him who sent me."

How did Christ yield his will to God? Maybe the most dramatic example of Christ yielding his will to God can be seen leading up to his crucifixion.

Luke 22:42
"Father, if you are willing, remove this cup from me. Nevertheless, not my will, but yours, be done."

Here is an obvious example of Jesus yielding his will to God. Of course, Jesus didn't want to experience the torture, humiliation, and death that he knew was coming. However, he ultimately wanted God's plan to come to fruition and he wanted our salvation. So, he yielded the desires of his flesh to accomplish the goals of the kingdom.

As Jesus kept God's commands and yielded his will to him, we are told to yield our will to Christ. This is the concept behind Christ telling us that we must take up our cross and follow him. That we are to die to ourselves. Or as Paul says, we are to be living sacrifices. We are giving God our lives to accomplish his goals for the kingdom through us.

Why would somebody give up everything like this? It is because they understand that while they are losing the desires of their flesh, they are gaining riches in all of eternity.

This is the personal gain that comes through obedience, but our obedience should be grounded in more than what we get out of it. Our obedience to God is a reflection of our love for God.

Chapter 14
God's Love Language

For the first couple of years of my marriage, I was not a great gift giver to my wife. As a matter of fact, I was pretty terrible at picking out a gift that expressed what I wanted it to express. Before you start thinking that my wife was just ungrateful, let me give you an example.

We had been married for less than a year and my wife's birthday was coming up, and I was feeling the pressure. I wanted to knock this out of the park. The only problem I had was that I had absolutely no idea what she might want. So, while I was trying to come up with a killer gift idea, I overheard her on the phone with a friend explaining to her this thing that she has been wanting.

This was it! How could I be so lucky? I secretly took note of what she wanted and proudly went out and made the purchase the next time I had the chance. I was confident, even while she was opening her gift, that I had done a good job.

However, to my surprise it didn't quite go the way I wanted it to. Apparently, a mop, no matter how fancy it is or how much she even wanted it, did not quite convey the message I wanted it to.

I wanted to say, "I cherish you," but what she heard was, "go clean the kitchen."

You can see the problem with this, right?

It wasn't that I didn't care, and it wasn't that I didn't try. Actually, I stressed over it way more than I do now. The root problem was that I didn't know my wife very well.

Fast forward many years, and I am a much better gift giver to my wife because now I know her. I know what makes her tick, so to speak. Usually in any given circumstance I know what she is thinking, and I can often anticipate what she will say next. Because I know her so well, I better understand the message a particular gift would send. I better know how to express my love to my wife.

Our relationship to God is very similar in many ways. Scripture often speaks to the importance of knowing God. One of the reasons Christ came to earth was so that we could "see the Father," so we would better understand God's heart and what he desires from us. I want us to look at some words of Christ on this topic, but first let's back up a bit.

God establishes very early that his desire is to be the God of his people. Obviously, he is God, but he desires that we put him in his rightful place and honor him as we should.

Look at the first three of the Ten Commandments. They all have to do with God's people honoring him as God.

What is one of the roles of God? To be in charge and in control. Fueled by our evil desires, we have the tendency to replace God with others or ourselves so that we can call the shots.

I wonder how many people try to please God with church attendance, or by checking this or that religious box, but ultimately, they do not have God on the throne.

If you know God, you know how he feels about that.

Matthew 15:8
"This people honors me with their lips, but their heart is far from me;"

We can do all sorts of religious activities, but are we expressing our love for God through our full obedience?

I know this is a long passage, but I want you to notice how consistently Christ ties our obedience to our love for him and God.

John 14:15-24
"If you love me, you will keep my commandments. And I will ask the Father, and he will give you another

Helper, to be with you forever, even the Spirit of truth, whom the world cannot receive, because it neither sees him nor knows him. You know him, for he dwells with you and will be in you. "I will not leave you as orphans; I will come to you. Yet a little while and the world will see me no more, but you will see me. Because I live, you also will live. In that day you will know that I am in my Father, and you in me, and I in you. Whoever has my commandments and keeps them, he it is who loves me. And he who loves me will be loved by my Father, and I will love him and manifest myself to him." Judas (not Iscariot) said to him, "Lord, how is it that you will manifest yourself to us, and not to the world?" Jesus answered him, "If anyone loves me, he will keep my word, and my Father will love him, and we will come to him and make our home with him. Whoever does not love me does not keep my words. And the word that you hear is not mine but the Father's who sent me.

We could go all over scripture to talk about this concept, but this one passage leaves us with the inescapable understanding that God desires that we love him through our obedience, and that he draws near to those who do.

Remember, we are ultimately after fellowship with God. It is our relationship with God which is to be the lens by which we are to see salvation. Scripture is clear that it is our fellowship with Christ and with God that brings about eternal life, and Jesus says that we draw near to God with obedience and he in return draws near to us.

The more we get to know God through his word we see that his love language is obedience.

God does not force himself on us. He wants us to have eternal life. He wants us to be in fellowship with him, but he wants us to want these things as well. He desires that we choose him like he has chosen us. God loves us and it is his wish that we love him in return.

How do we best express our love for God? By obeying his will.

Obedience will take you places you would not go on your own. This is because you are yielding your will to God. You will make decisions and say things that you would not say if you were just protecting your worldly interests. Therefore, obedience will sometimes put you in tough situations that will cause you to lose worldly status or even friends and family members. It may even lead to persecution.

1 John 5:3
For this is the love of God, that we keep his commandments. And his commandments are not burdensome.

First, notice that our love is again connected to our obedience.

Secondly, how come Christ calls for such devotion to his will that it could cost us our very lives, and at the same time scripture says his commands are not burdensome? How can that be the case?

The answer to that question is that again we must see this through the lens of relationship.

As parents, my wife and I are responsible for providing for and taking care of our children. We have changed thousands of diapers and stayed up all night with crying babies. We have worked hours and hours to put food on the table to sustain their lives. However, do you think that we feel burdened by taking care of them? No, they are our kids. We want to take care of them. Their sustenance and success are now our personal goal as well. Because we love them like we do, I do not see any of it as a burden.

I think it is to be the same way in our obedience to God. We love him so much that we begin to desire what God desires. We begin to share in his mission and so our obedience is not burdensome. While it sometimes may be uncomfortable to follow God's will, it is not a burden when you love whom you serve.

Those things we do for God should be done from a place of love and devotion. This is the way God wants it to be. He wants you to keep his commands not out of obligation alone, but because you love him and have aligned your desires to match up with his. I believe this is what Jesus was getting at when he said that loving God was the greatest command and that loving each other was like it. The things we do for God or for others in the name of Christ should not be viewed as merely religious, but as a relationship. We are not just checking boxes; we are honoring and loving God with our good deeds. Jesus says that the law and the prophets, which is shorthand for all of God's commands to them in the Bible, depend on these two commands. Meaning, that all the things God has told us to do for him or for others, should be motivated from that love we are to have.

This is how we maintain that connection to Christ, by being obedient through love.

Chapter 15

That You May Know

One of the most telling symptoms of the masses not understanding the new covenant, is that you have many Christians walking around unsure of their salvation. While some feel the most humble approach is to act as if they don't know if they will go to heaven or not, this is not what God wants for his people. This is not how he wants his people to live their lives. It is God's desire for us to know that we have salvation, and that it is not a confidence in our own ability to save ourselves nor is it a confidence born out of blind faith. There is a way we can know, and it is dependent on our understanding of how the New Covenant is designed to work.

We spent a lot of time in John 15 as we talked about what it means to abide in Christ. As you remember, using vines and branches, Jesus gives us an illustration which helps us wrap our minds around the relationship we are to have with Christ, which gives us life. In this discussion, Jesus brings up the concept that we need to understand if we want to know that we have spiritual life. Jesus says we can prove it.

John 15:8
"By this my Father is glorified, that you bear much fruit and so prove to be my disciples."

Previously in the text, Jesus explained that the only way that you as a branch will produce fruit, is if you are connected to the vine. This is a great illustration because we get it. If a branch's life is dependent on being connected to the vine, then it's ability to produce fruit is certainly dependent on that connection as well. Jesus is saying that fruit will only be produced in your life if you are in that relationship with Christ that also brings about life. In other words, if you have eternal life because of your connection to Christ, there will also be something visible in your life which "proves" that connection.

If the fruit is the proof, then we need to understand what this fruit is so we know what we are looking for. If I had to distill the New Testament definition of fruit, I would simply define it as Christ-like changes in your life that impacts the kingdom. However, I think it is important to see how the Bible handles the imagery of fruit because it will add to our understanding of how we can know that we have life.

Galatians 5:22-24

But the fruit of the Spirit is love, joy, peace, patience, kindness, goodness, faithfulness, gentleness, self-control; against such things there is no law. And those who belong to Christ Jesus have crucified the flesh with its passions and desires.

The idea is that these traits are Godly traits; they are fruit of the Spirit. The Spirit is God, Jesus is God, and the Father is God. So, the fruit of the Spirit is the production of these God-like traits in your life. Notice how he ties all of this to our belonging to Christ; this relationship status we have been discussing.

Fruit production in your life makes you more like God. This is important to know. Jesus gives us a good example of fruit production which makes us more like him and is proof of our connection to him in John 13.

John 13:34-35

"A new commandment I give to you, that you love one another: just as I have loved you, you also are to love one another. By this all people will know that you are my disciples, if you have love for one another."

Jesus tells his disciples he has a new commandment for them. He tells them to love one another. However, to love each other is not a new command. They were told to love their neighbors in the law, so why does Jesus say this is a new command? It is a new command because Christ has newly and narrowly defined the love they are to show each other. What is the definition of this love?

117

It is himself, how he loved them. Until Christ lived, and more importantly, died on the cross for his disciples, this command could not be understood.

(Side note: The world has a working definition of the word love, but Jesus' definition is different and specific. The fruit Jesus talks about is God-defined through scripture. We don't get to define what the fruit is.)

Remember that we said this fruit that is produced in our lives makes us more like Christ or God. Well, Jesus here is telling them to exhibit this trait or quality that would make them more like him and notice what the outcome is when this takes place. *"By this all people will **know** that you are my disciples..."*

See how there is this inherent proof of connection to Christ when we begin to exhibit these traits in our lives? Not only for ourselves but even to others as well. This proof of connection to Christ also operates as proof of eternal life for us. This only works when we understand how new covenant salvation has been designed. When we understand that it is our connection to Christ that saves us, then and only then does this proof of connection also equal proof of life.

I love how Peter talks about this concept in such a matter-of-fact way, he doesn't use any illustrations or imagery. He just talks about this principle in a very straightforward manner.

2 peter 1:3-11
His divine power has granted to us all things that pertain to life and godliness, through the knowledge

of him who called us to his own glory and excellence, by which he has granted to us his precious and very great promises, so that through them you may become partakers of the divine nature, having escaped from the corruption that is in the world because of sinful desire. For this very reason, make every effort to supplement your faith with virtue, and virtue with knowledge, and knowledge with self-control, and self-control with steadfastness, and steadfastness with godliness, and godliness with brotherly affection, and brotherly affection with love. For if these qualities are yours and are increasing, they keep you from being ineffective or unfruitful in the knowledge of our Lord Jesus Christ. For whoever lacks these qualities is so nearsighted that he is blind, having forgotten that he was cleansed from his former sins. Therefore, brothers, be all the more diligent to confirm your calling and election, for if you practice these qualities you will never fall. For in this way there will be richly provided for you an entrance into the eternal kingdom of our Lord and Savior Jesus Christ.

He begins by saying that we have been enabled to *be partakers of the divine nature*. What does this mean? Everything has its own nature. A dog behaves like a dog, it is their nature. A human does human things because it is in their nature to be human. God has a nature as well. What is Peter saying when he says we can be partakers in the divine nature? He says that we have been given the opportunity to do something amazing. We get to do something that does not naturally happen;

we get to shed our human nature and start picking up the nature of God. To say it simply, we can become more like God. This sounds familiar, right? This is what fruit production in our life does. It makes us more like God. Peter is talking about this very same concept. He is just approaching it without the imagery of fruit and is talking about it in a very straightforward way.

Look at verse 10. He says that when we add these traits and qualities then we confirm our calling and election. This completely coincides with what Christ says. When fruit is produced in our life, then it is obvious that we have this connection to Christ, and connection to Christ is what gives us life.

Satan and the world are not going to help you become like Christ, so when you do start to become like Christ, it is obvious that this only comes from him. Christ is the only vine that produces God-like fruit. This is why it inspires our confidence in salvation.

If you want to do a bible study about being confident in your salvation, I would start with 1 John. This is one of the major reasons John writes this letter.

1 John 5:13
I write these things to you who believe in the name of the Son of God, that you may know that you have eternal life.

First of all, we cannot escape the fact that it is not only possible, but that it is important that we know we have salvation. This is one of the main purposes for writing a book of the New Testament.

So how does John say that we can know that we have eternal life?

If I were to sum up how he handles this topic, it will sound very familiar to what we have seen so far. He confirms that our fellowship with Christ is what brings about life and that you can test your fellowship with Christ by the presence, or lack of, Christ-like traits and qualities in your life. He gives a series of fellowship tests so that the reader can do some self-reflection and determine if they are a branch connected to the vine or not.

Previously we discussed how Jesus said that our obedience to his teachings maintains this life-giving connection to Christ. It only makes sense that our obedience to his teachings is going to produce spiritual fruit in our lives. This fruit production is something that we can see as confirmation that we are in fellowship with him, and if we are bearing fruit because we are connected to the vine, then we also know that we have life.

We know that we have life because we know that we have fellowship with Christ.

Many who have bought into all of today's deception will tell you that you just need to have a blind faith in your salvation, but this is never how the scripture handles this topic. God wants you to know by having evidence. He wants your confidence to be inspired by something tangible and real. He doesn't want you to desperately hold on to some false confidence, he wants you to have the real thing. The real thing is found when we correctly understand and engage in the New Covenant plan God has designed.

Eternal life comes through being in fellowship with Christ, or in other words, being **in Christ**. God, through his word, outlines how we engage in and maintain that life-giving relationship with Jesus. When you are connected to, or are abiding in Jesus, then and only then will you be producing the fruit of God, or as Peter says, partaking of the divine nature. When you can see this progression of God-like traits and qualities in your life, then you can know or have confidence in your salvation. Why? Because the fruit of the Spirit is only produced in the lives of those who are connected to the vine of Christ, and those who are connected to the vine have life.

Do you have this fellowship with Christ which brings about life? Some of you know that you do. Wonderful! Some of you know that you don't. If you do not, I urge you to engage God in a relationship the way that he has designed for us to.

Maybe you find yourself somewhere in between these groups. Maybe you are not sure if you have this fellowship with God which gives life. This is an understandable place to find yourself in today's church. Deception has muddied the clear waters of God's plan.

If you are unsure, then I think you need to treat this

uncertainty as a symptom of a bigger spiritual problem. Don't just try to blindly reassure yourself. Scripture plainly says that God's people should have confidence based on tangible evidence of their relationship with God.

You will find this evidence in the fruit produced in your life which only comes by being connected to the vine which is Christ. The only way you connect to the vine is when you pursue God in relationship through your obedience to his ordained way.

John 17:3
"And this is eternal life, that they know you, the only true God, and Jesus Christ whom you have sent."

Chapter 16

Count the Cost

While I desperately wish that everyone would go to heaven and nobody would experience hell, I am not going to beg you to become a Christian. It was Jesus' mission to seek and save the lost and you never see him begging people to become disciples. Why is that? That is because nobody becomes a true disciple of Christ because they feel obligated, or because they were coaxed into it. Maybe this seems possible by how our religious culture defines what it means to be a disciple of Christ. Mainstream Christianity puts out the vibe that if you would just say the right words or do the right initial process, then you are in God's grace, and nothing can take away that salvation no matter what you do after that. As we have established earlier, this is not how Jesus or the New Testament deals with the concept of salvation. Jesus makes it very clear that his disciples are those who are willing to sacrifice everything to serve him. You don't have to beg someone to become a disciple of Christ if that person would give up everything to make it happen. Let's look at one of the many places where Jesus lays out his expectations for his disciples.

Luke 14:25-33

Now great crowds accompanied him, and he turned and said to them, "If anyone comes to me and does not hate his own father and mother and wife and children and brothers and sisters, yes, and even his own life, he cannot be my disciple. Whoever does not bear his own cross and come after me cannot be my disciple. For which of you, desiring to build a tower, does not first sit down and count the cost, whether he has enough to complete it? Otherwise, when he has laid a foundation and is not able to finish, all who see it begin to mock him, saying, 'This man began to build and was not able to finish.' Or what king, going out to encounter another king in war, will not sit down first and deliberate whether he is able with ten thousand to meet him who comes against him with twenty thousand? And if not, while the other is yet a great way off, he sends a delegation and asks for terms of peace. So therefore, any one of you who does not renounce all that he has cannot be my disciple."

First of all, Jesus is not saying that we should literally hate anybody. As a matter of fact, this is the same Jesus who said we should love our enemies. It wouldn't make sense that he would then say we should turn around and hate our families. Instead, Jesus is using a teaching device here that he often uses, and to keep from going too far off subject, let's just say that his goal is to cause his listeners to somewhat struggle with what he says, so that they will then work and dig to figure out what he means.

Jesus wants us to understand that in order to be his disciple we must give him our full allegiance. There is not anything that you have or anyone that you know who should keep you from fully serving Christ. Your allegiance and devotion to Jesus must come first, above all. Even above yourself.

Three times Jesus makes the unequivocal pronouncement that unless you meet the requirement that he states, you cannot be his disciple. You can find those in verses 26, 27, and 33. I just want to quickly sum up what he is saying here in these verses.

Verse 26: If you want to be Jesus' disciple then nobody can come before your devotion to Christ and his will for your life, not even those who you will naturally love the most.

Verse 27: If you want to be Jesus' disciple then your devotion to him needs to even exceed your devotion to yourself.

Verse 33: If you want to be Jesus' disciple then nothing should come before him.

Because all these requirements exist for Jesus' disciples, he says that we should count the cost before we decide to follow him. We should weigh whether or not we are willing to commit to him on this level. Jesus is setting expectations for what it means to be his disciple and it is far different than what mainstream Christianity tends to push. Jesus is not calling for us to live our lives essentially how we want to, and just throw a little Jesus in the mix to make ourselves feel better about eternity. No, he says that unless we are fully committed, we cannot be his disciple. I want us to look at another place where he sets expectations like this.

Matthew 16:24-25
Then Jesus told his disciples, "If anyone would come after me, let him deny himself and take up his cross and follow me. For whoever would save his life will lose it, but whoever loses his life for my sake will find it."

Again, Jesus is talking about the commitment level he expects from his disciples and what does Jesus expect? Our martyrdom.

He expects his disciples to be willing to die for him and for the cause. Now, you will probably never have to die for Jesus in the sense that somebody puts a gun to your head, and you have to make a decision at that moment if you will die for Christ or not. However, he calls each of his disciples to be martyrs because he calls each of his disciples to live for him. In that way, we all give our lives for Christ. We take the life that we would live, and we give that all up and pursue Christ's will for our lives instead. If you ever wonder how you would handle a life-or-death situation and if you would die for Christ or not, a good indication is if you are truly living for him or not now. It is in that way, all of Jesus' disciples are martyrs.

We could go on and on through the teachings of Christ and look at these types of expectations that he places on his disciples. However, I feel like we can see in just these two passages that what mainstream Christianity calls us to, and what Christ calls us to, are two different things. Always make sure you are following Christ and not the ways of man.

We have established that in order to be Christ's disciples that we must be his sacrificial servants. Why are you or I willing to do this?

Matthew 19:29-30
And everyone who has left houses or brothers or sisters or father or mother or children or lands, for my name's sake, will receive a hundredfold and will inherit eternal life. But many who are first will be last, and the last first.

Jesus says that those who sacrifice for the sake of Jesus and the kingdom will receive a hundredfold more than what they gave up and will receive eternal life. Those who become sacrificial servants for Christ and his kingdom will be the ones lifted up in the end.

Unless somebody has faith in eternity, they would never be a disciple of Christ. This is another reason it is not effective to beg people to become a disciple. If a person never gives any thought to eternity, why would they give up this life to become a disciple? Only those who understand what Jesus means when he says, "But many who are first will be last, and the last first," would commit themselves in such a way. We need to know that all we endure and all that we give up here will be worth it in the end. It reminds me of the words of Paul to the believers in Rome.

Romans 8:16-18
The Spirit himself bears witness with our spirit that we are children of God, and if children, then heirs—heirs of God and fellow heirs with Christ, provided we suffer with him in order that we may also be glorified with him.
For I consider that the sufferings of this present time are not worth comparing with the glory that is to be revealed to us.

Whatever it is we must give up or endure for the name of Christ is absolutely nothing compared to what we will be receiving in eternity. This is what a person must know and understand before they are willing to commit themselves in this manner.

All of this being said, I am concerned about your eternity, but I am not going to beg you to be a Christian. Instead, I am going to merely ask you to consider what is going to happen after you die. It doesn't matter what this or that group of people think, it matters what is true and real, and I think that deep down, at least at some point, all people know there is an eternity. As it is said, eternity is written on our hearts.

If you find yourself in this place where you believe in eternity and believe in Christ, then I hope this book is merely a tool that points you to the truth of the scripture, and you will establish a relationship with Christ that leads to life.

www.ingramcontent.com/pod-product-compliance
Lightning Source LLC
Chambersburg PA
CBHW061956040426
42447CB00028B/2864